The Blood of Words

To my father, **Chuck Stone,**
*the one person in life
who showed me unconditional love.*

The Blood of Words

SHANE STONE

PRIMIX
PUBLISHING
THE WRITE CHOICE

Primix Publishing
11620 Wilshire Blvd
Suite 900, West Wilshire Center, Los Angeles, CA, 90025
www.primixpublishing.com
Phone: 1-800-538-5788

© 2022 Shane Stone. All rights reserved.

No part of this book may be reproduced, stored in a retrieval system, or transmitted by any means without the written permission of the author.

Published by Primix Publishing   10/18/2022

ISBN: 978-1-955944-22-9(sc)
ISBN: 979-8-887030-84-5(hc)
ISBN: 978-1-955944-23-6(e)

Library of Congress Control Number: 2021921146

Any people depicted in stock imagery provided by iStock are models, and such images are being used for illustrative purposes only.

Certain stock imagery © iStock.

Because of the dynamic nature of the Internet, any web addresses or links contained in this book may have changed since publication and may no longer be valid. The views expressed in this work are solely those of the author and do not necessarily reflect the views of the publisher, and the publisher hereby disclaims any responsibility for them.

Contents

The Blood of Words 1
Visions 17
The Blue Dark Light 20
The Madness it Takes to Evolve 25
Madness Seems Needed 27
The Hanged Man 29
Song of the Hanged Man 32
The Gates of the Crypt 33
Highway Man's Song 34
The Song of the Wolf 35
The Time to Stand 38
The Kingdom of Stars 39
Prayers of Tears 41
Dark Confession 42
To the Dark Magicians 43
The Phantom of Song 45
The Monster of Love 47
Risen from the Grave 48
The Burning Forest 49
Lost Eden 50
Looking for a New World 53
Blue 54
Immortal Love 56
Birthing Monsters 57
Shadows of Night and Memory 58
Ode to Death 60

The Gray Rider	62
Sublime Dreams Creeping In	64
A Strange Dream	66
Dead Dream	68
Faded Seasons	69
Heart in a Cage	70
Dead Heart Beats	72
Dead Man in the Mirror	74
Tired	75
Ashes to Ashes	76
Tale to Tell	77
Fallen Angel's Song	78
Nature's Call	79
Unspoken Sound	80
Opening the Ancient Darkness	82
Dawn at Midnight	83
Life with Death at My Side	85
It Dawned on Me	86
Moments in Time	87
Ghost	88
Gray	89
Faded Roses	90
Relic	91
The Breadcrumbs of Sanity	92
The Bewilderment	93
Questions of Reincarnation	94
Waking the Anti-Hero	95
Time to Rise	97
The Rebirth Spoken	99
The Mind Wars	102
Becoming Aware	105
The Awakening of Melancholia	111
The Adventures of Melancholia	115
The Further Adventures of Melancholia	117

The Blood of Words

What Morbid Creatures are these who Cast a Deal for the Promise of Words? Those longed for by the Tongue of Spoken Delight, in payment for the Essence of Life

They come offering Gifts of the Sublime, a Riddle of Fame

Here from the Shadow of Souls they offer the Bride of Poets

For Acts of Blood and Murder they would reward with the Admiration of the World

Come into the Din of Darkness, into the Flame of Desire, and hear a Tale of Madness

Found liable to pay the Ego of the Damned, the pages hunger in their Blankness of Words

Time to feed them, for the Desires of the Flesh call to them from Years of Woe

Bringing the tears of those who must pay to create them, they come through dreams, tearing at my flesh, grasping at my Soul

Daring me to cross over into the Abyss, they promise Wisdom derived from Torments, the likes of which have never before been seen

Do I dare trade a Plight of Pain for Knowledge of the Great Beyond?

They lead not to Heaven but to a Place without Light

A Place only dreamt of by Living Man

They offer a Stairway into Horror, into a Place where None Return

They do beckon, they call to me, but I linger, only staring into their somber faces

Knowing that to enter may result in my Utter Damnation, thus ahead lie the Gates of Hell

Yet these Creatures of Night seduce me with their Gaze of Shadows

Shall I pay them what they ask? They promise the World and all its Desire

Oh, to finally be heard after a Lifetime in Exile, without Love, without Feelings, how long has it been since I was remembered?

Yes, I shall enter, I must know, I must enter the Realm of Lament

Let me hear your Offer---to debate the Devil---to hear his side of the Story

So I may share his Song of Sorrowful Descent, my King of Torments, share with me your chains

I long to know your depths of Divine Suffering, not as Confederate Member, but as one willing to tell with Sympathy your Fall from Grace

May God forgive my Story of the Father of Darkness, but there are so few willing to hear with Empathy the Tale of one so great's Plunge from Glory

I take my pen to compose his Beautiful Banishment, so as to find the reason a Heart so pure could become a Mountain of the Blackest Coal

Reaching out into the Universe to those he sees fit to reveal the Infinite Grasp of True Darkness

He has chosen to take my own Self as a Payment for entry, but I have purposed within my own Wits to keep my Soul off of the Bargaining Table

Yet I must in Absolute Certainty come forth to grant him Respect

Making also an Altar of his Misunderstood Plight to the Lovers of the Righteous Paths

Thereby giving Reason to a Road taken into Gloom and Exile

It would be crossed by the only One daring enough to walk alone into the Realm of Chaos and Darkness

And as he did, he fashioned a Crown out of the embers, and from the brimstone he constructed a Throne, something befitting this Palace of the Unknown that he now calls Home

All comforts do now lie at my beck and call as long as I can find a way to show the World that the Prince of Darkness is simply a Victim of Circumstance

After all, every Story has to have a Villain

Here in his House of Ill Repute that caters to every Lust of the Flesh, the cost is a worry not to be pondered, the Payment will come later, as such details are of little importance he explains

He says, "Let us not be concerned with such matters, let us discuss the Weather and fair Songs of gray clouds turned to blue by the Tempest of a Fallen Angel's Eye, let us witness a Dance composed for the Damned"

Grand is the Ballroom, and the Costumes of Flesh offer the Illusion of Glamour

And such is Beauty, for it hides the disfigured Souls within

I do not offer my Soul, only my aid in sharing this Fallen Star's perspective with those he longs to reach

The Suffering here is Biblical, and as one who has tasted True Torment (though only from its Outskirts), I am willing to endure the stench of brimstone for a Story few would dare to pursue

What a Burden our Son of Perdition carries, riding his Nightmare Stead across the Scattered Ruins that reveal Desolate Highways forged by the Jaded Minds of a Self-Destructive Mankind

We joined his ranks with our smited Wars of Envy, Guilty as any self-proclaimed Godhead, we have become as bold as the Dark Angel himself, "so as to proclaim ourselves Gods"

No longer in need of any Faith, save that of the Faith of Man-Made Gods, believing only in the Appetite of Our Own Lusts

With Technology we have replaced our Spiritual needs, so as to build a new Tower of Babel, so that we may enter into Heaven even though uninvited

There are few on Earth who have not committed Sins worthy of Damnation, so I think it best to find some Sympathy for the Lord of the Damned

The name Jesus is to be spoken softly here, but he is your best Chance if you find yourself in need of a Lawyer

That is, if we should find ourselves Fallen from Grace, having taken part in the same Prideful Follies as God's once Most-Beloved Angel

Should any of us happen to Repent, we might gain a Pardon, yet I must end this mention of Repentance for my Host seems to be saying something about tearing my Heart out and feeding it to me if I talk of such things again

He really does have some of the greatest of Entertainers, and the Social Life here would make the most lavish of Hollywood Parties turn green with Envy, although they do seem to be very much the same

Yes Hollywood-Babylon is a place he visits often, enticing the Up-And-Coming with Fame, and for the mere price of what little Soul they have left, he gives them the Admiration they so desire

Although he says he sickens at the Award Shows, with everyone there thanking God

He feels left out when no one thanks him for the Inspiration he grants them

But he says, "No matter", for he has all the Time in the Universe to torment those Ungrateful Lushes

He seems to like me, he says I remind him of one of God's Older Works, an Angel whom he had persuaded to join him in his Uprising and eventual Fall

"We seem to have the same distaste for Man", he says, and that is why he has allowed me to tell his Story

For I myself see Man as little more than a Beast having been given Speech, an Upright Ape who gave up the Divine to pursue his own desire for Mortal Pleasure

What little Imagination we have, I long to roam the galaxies, to see the unseen

Although Earth has its moments, I still remember the Tears of Love that flowed like oceans, yet now they are but deserts I've crossed in the Valley of Death

When I left I gave Black Roses to the woman who had waited for so long to be my Bride

I left my Lady of the Grave with all of the salt that my tears had once made, and flew on in search of other Worlds

Hell is always open, so here I sit, contemplating the Fate of a World that has passed beyond the Point of No Return

Having asked my Host what the Future holds, he laughed, saying, "Sit back and enjoy the Show, th Apocalypse is coming to a theater near you!"

He seems resentful that he has been forgotten, so I tell him, "Give them Time, not everyone has forgotten you"

But he sees his Followers as Half-Hearted, they are not worthy of his Admiration, they don't enjoy Pain as much as he

I tell him even I enjoy Pleasure at least once every thousand years

It was at this point that he forced me into a chair, had me remove my own eyes and he then proceeded to feed them to me, asking me if the seasoning was to my liking

Well, to my Painful Delight they were quite tasty

But then to my Horror, he drove spikes into my sockets, and then managed to return my Sight while at the same time making a jest that I had "something in my eye"

After a short lifetime (about that of a Rockstar), he returned me to my former state, claiming I had amused him, and suggested that we continue his Story

To say the least, I began writing again very quickly

He couldn't understand why I was not Afraid like so many before me

I told him of my Search for Wisdom, how even at the Price of Sorrow I had felt compelled to sail through the greatest of storms

Maybe we were more alike than I had first thought, for the following account provides his Reasoning for his Rejection of Repentance---he told me how he had stood by God's Side, obeying every Command, yet God had demoted him

So he started an Uprising that lead to the inevitable War in Heaven

Within his Fall from Grace he searched for Meaning, he searched for an Attainment of Wisdom that could equal God's own

He forced his way through the Gates of Chaos and the Darkness of Hell, casting Sin and Death aside with a shrug

He searched the Universe for its Absolutes of Truth and he overcame his Doubt with his own Pride---for he alone was Brave enough to test God's Wrath again

Even after falling so far, even after having fallen for so long, God had still left his Will intact

He had removed him from his Presence but had left him to serve a Purpose

After all, how can there be Good without Evil? The Laws of the Universe must be kept, even by God

They cannot be changed, they must be paid

Lucifer was reluctant to share such Wisdom, it seemed I may now be learning too much for my own Good

I told him I had no intention of trying to fill his shoes, much less putting my hat in the ring for his Job

I told him I was strictly in need of his side of the Story, after all, God doesn't grace many with his Presence, personally, so I had to come to him to gain knowledge

At this point he removed my flesh layer by layer, slowly stripping me to the bone

In the most painful of Agonies he then lead me to a Golden Door

He said, "Behind this Door is a Library, this is where I keep the Books of Wisdom that mortals desire, feel free to peruse the Wisdom you seek, but you must remain in the painful state you're now in until you either give up your Thirst for Knowledge or quench it through a pain heretofore undreamt of by the Living"

I read on till I had almost finished reading the contents of the vast halls, then he removed me by Force, saying, "I didn't expect you to endure so long, you've been in there for ten thousand years and I can't have you knowing all of my Secrets"

He then returned my flesh and provided me an Invitation to Dinner

He said, "We will debate what you have learned over a Great Feast"

The Wine was sublime and every manner of Lusts of the Flesh was brought out as Appetizers

The Desires of the Universe came forth as the Last Course before Dessert

I had consumed a whole Pie of Understanding before I was told the Feast had concluded

It was time for a discussion, and After-Dinner drinks were brought in

I found the Benediction to be most appetizing but I was inevitably asked what I had learned

Over an Endless Platter of the most divine drinks, I confessed, "Wisdom is without end, there is no way of knowing everything, the Fruits of Wisdom ripen with fresh blooms Eternally, so how could one find Knowledge equal to God?"

He smiled with delight, as if I had struck the very chord he had longed for me to play

He said, "Naturally! The only way to know the Mind of God is to become him, as that has been my Pursuit all along"

He looked at me with interest, saying, "Now you must help me fulfil this Madness"

Needless to say, this set me a little off balance

I understood his Desire, but could find no way to grant it

I think he had forgotten the fact that I was merely a Man

He wanted my help to overthrow Heaven

It seems after all this Time in Eternity he still dreamt of being its new King

I dared not question how he could still think such a thing possible

If Wisdom's seeds grow Eternally, how could one Hope to gain its Infinite Truth?

All of a sudden, a Businessman arrived

He was ushered through the Gates and all the Wealth he had gathered on Earth was placed on his back, crushing his bones instantly

He lay there in a pile of gold and blood and was told he would carry his Riches as a Burden for all Eternity

Diamonds were driven into his flesh and he was then formed into a spineless worm

He crawled off into the Darkness while my companion laughed hysterically, saying, "Enjoy your retirement!"

This Cosmic Justice seems to weigh on us all, but I could only Hope my Wits would allow me to delay receiving a similar Fate, to the extent that I could still manage to Amuse

In this Desolate Kingdom, all Roads come to Dead Ends

They lead to Mires that pull the Soul down

This is a King of Madness, yet his Charisma is overwhelming

He seems to be forging me into the Unspoken Creature I've always been, yet even now I long for a Candle of Hope

This Dark Chamber has overcome me, shall I join the Ranks of the Damned?

Forever serving as Herald here to the Twilight, I decay in Mind but not in Spirit

I take on the Shroud of Gloom to know the Wisdom of Sorrow

This Isolation is a burdensome Crown, yet my Suffering brings Knowledge from the Cup of the Divine

Here lies the Heavy Goblet

Is it better to Sleep or to Awaken?

I am among the few who have dared to look behind Life's Meaning

Do I stand now ushered beyond the Curtain because I have seen too much?

Perhaps it is Poetic Justice to be left marooned, alone with no one to speak to regarding the Words I so longed to learn

Nevertheless, I shall keep my Faith with God, after all I have seen it is better to hold on to what little Good I have kept, rather than to continue building my Tower of Doom

I must discard a portion of my Selfish Tongue! I must find Reason beyond the Madness of the Infinite

Can I find my way back through this Crypt to the Land of the Living, or am I to become a Specter, am I to be no more than a Living Ghost?

I would speak and declare to the Universe, "I have found more in the Loss of Love than mere Regret, I have found that its Momentary Glory at once delivers more than its often Tragic End could ever forsake"

I dare say I did love Life and all its Spirit. Through the Tempest I would yell, "Sail on through the Gray Lady! Ride the Three Sisters' Waves! And hold dear your companion's Lifeboat!"

In both Love and War it's possible to lose for the sake of Glory but only the Brave will taste the Truth of Life

Would you be willing to pay the price as I have to truly gain the Knowledge of Good and Evil?

Knowledge is Power but it comes with the Burden of Loneliness

My only Friends who are left and still stop by are Lucifer, Sam, and Jesus Christ

But how could I Hope the World would not find me Mad, having no evidence to present of such affairs?

Here I am drifting through Space and Time

Somewhere along the Milky Way I find a Black Hole

From there I venture through to find the Other Side of Reason, wherein states that this Place of the Infinite Universe is beyond Explanation

For I can only try to tell this Story by telling my own

Naked to the World, I sit High upon the Moor, watching Life pass by through a Stranger's Eyes

Here I sit debating God and his Old Friend the Prince of Darkness

I sit without company, save some old Songs, waiting for the youngest son of Jubal to sing a New Song, maybe something along the lines of *King David's Chord*

I wish I could sing this New Song to the World

Could this be why I'm still here? Could I still leave the World something to remember me by? Could I still share some Good here behind my Walls?

A Man can dream such things if he still believes in the Infinite

I can't be the only one who still believes in this Dream

Would anyone dare to join me out here singing to the Cosmos? These performances are beyond the Price of the World

This Song is not about Fame, it's about Redemption

All Myths hold a certain amount of Truth, the problem arises when One tries to separate Fact from Fiction, though

At that Time the Devil came in with a tray of drinks to add to the Melancholy within my Soul

He said, "Don't feel so down, let's talk for a while, I'll trade you Wealth and all that you desire for Songs of Sorrow and Lamentation"

I told him I would tell the World of his Offer, but that I had other Plans

I was looking for Songs of Bliss, for in my Eternal Sadness I still dreamt of Forgotten Shores, I still held a Thread of Hope

He then lept into my Mind in order to fill it with Horror

Images of Suffering Unimagined came flashing before my eyes

All that I Loved was taken from me and was Raped and Murdered as I watched in Helpless Agony

There now seemed to be nothing but Darkness throughout the entire Universe, so I searched on for Light

After what seemed a few lifetimes, I suddenly burst into a laughter that could not be contained

I found my body starting to glow with the Blinding Light that I had been searching for all along

It had been there the entire Time

It seemed I had broken through the Fabric of the Illusion of my Reality

Hell's Gates were finally fading from the rearview mirror of my Soul

I was Free, though unfortunately lost in Time and Space, but Free

So now I searched for a galaxy that I could call Home (whatever that is to me)

"Destroy!" The spirits cried, "Find Worlds and send them to Oblivion!"

I fled to escape the Wrath they had driven into the Structure of my Being

I needed rest, for the Horrors still haunted me

So I took the Hand of Madness in hopes of finding the Peace of Laughter

I returned to Earth to witness the Carnival of Man, a Freakshow called Society

It gave me comfort to see those who had not evolved

The Relics of Mind that had not seen beyond the Illusion of Life and Death's Vail

I laugh, smug in a drunken stupor with the occupants of the Abyss

This seemed an appropriate location to gather my Thoughts

But it was here that I found instead the Devil's Daughter

And due to her unfamiliarity with Pain, her screams gave respite to the Boredom that dwelt in the bottom of my Soul

She seemed to enjoy the suffering in my Heart

When we met she said, "Mortal, come and let us find a chamber so we may commune"

She wanted me to share with her my Wisdom, she wanted to know what it was like to be Mortal

She said, "Unleash your Shadow upon my Flesh", she wanted to taste my bitter tongue

"Chain me to your Tomb of Unmet Desires, let me feel the Savage Lust of all of your Cravings", she begged

I ravaged her in ways that were unknown even to her, I taught her things, and it was there that I showed her the true Meaning of Life

She cried, "No more! You have drained my Ego!"

She then retreated into a Throne Room and there began to drink her fill of Virgin Blood, saying, "You have pleased me Mortal, return again"

The Shadow of my Emptiness had won her Heart, but I left and went in search of God, for I now tired of the Desires of the Flesh

My quest lead me to become Exiled on a desert plane

And though the Devil's Daughter still lingered in my Mind and haunted my Dreams, I began to think of God's Desire

I wanted his Love, his Approval, so I began to Pray

I Prayed that he would Forgive me for my Sins, yet this troubled me, for I knew I would Sin again

But even if he never let me into Heaven, I would still Love him

So further across the desert I trudged, but only now it was with an Understanding of the True Value of Life

And this lead me to believe my Life was not mine to take, so my thoughts of Suicide were abandoned

Now I would fill the Void inside of me with a Knowledge of True Understanding

For Life is Priceless and Wisdom is Infinite

There is always something more to be learned, so I search the Universe forever for Teachers in order to become One with True Meaning

This is how I defeated the Horror of the Knowledge of Suffering within all Worlds

But alas! It drives me Insane with Reason---this endless Hunger for Truth and Life

I then spread my wings to Fly but instead fell into a Cascade of Blinding Shimmering Light

I thought the Light would rob me of my Sight, but the Black Void refused to allow my Descent into Time

It was then that I tasted Tears of Lament watering my tongue

And as I was once again pulled into a Freefall Dive, I stared down the Spiral of Winding Descent

From here I could see the Soulless Shadows of the Tormented, they were Dancing into the Arms of Chaos

I needed rest so I fell asleep in the Bosom of Wisdom's Argument

I also needed Time to Think

I began to paint the galaxy with Blood, the Blood of Poets

Creating a Vision of Dawn that was worthy of the gaze of those witnessing from below

It was a painting of Enlightenments

I dreamt of casting Light into the Hopeless Eyes of the myriads who wailed miles below

Though I was alone I found Strength in the Nest of Wisdom

I came to enjoy painting the skies for the Damned, I watched them gather to view the Dawns I had made

I had finally found Ones who loved my works as much as I

When the Devil found out what I had done he cast me out

Into a Great Void I fell silently beyond the Edge of Hope, but it was there that it occurred to me to plot a new course

How can I escape this Isolation? Even the Prince of Darkness has Exiled me

I began to Pray to God, I Prayed he would finally answer me

He appeared after many lifetimes had passed by

The Void had prepared me for his Presence

He told me, "I give you the Power to make your own Worlds, for in you I have found some Worth, do not disappoint me as you have in the past, imbue your Creations with the Hope you provided to the Damned while living in the Nest of Wisdom's Argument, your Blood's Hope will be the Light in the Eyes of the clouds you create, the Words that bleed from your Heart will turn green the mountains that form along your Foothold, you must Sacrifice your own Joy to make the stars that Light the Way to my Kingdom, if you do this I may let you enter in due Time, now go and do not question my Judgment, this is your Debt, the Universal Laws must be obeyed!"

With my Blood I painted the skies with the blue hues of Song Birds, I made trees of purple and oceans of yellow sunflowers, there were snowflakes of orange sunshine and white tigers that roamed the fields of red roses, wolves took to the cliffs and guarded the Doors of the Dead, I looked to the ravens to ensnare the serpents that longed to know my World, there were no Humans to whom I gave passage, I did not want this World ruined before it had begun, I made star fruit on fig trees to feed the animals, bright sunbeams I made from the Light that I knew still existed in my Heart, my tears became lakes, rivers, and even oceans that quenched the thirst of all I had Created

It was then that I felt the true Loneliness of God, for I longed to have someone to confide in but had found none Worthy

I needed someone Pure but found only emptiness in my pursuit of a Mate

So I opened the Gates of the Galaxies, and in graveyards I searched for a kindred Spirit

There in the midst of an Ancient Fog I found the True Angel of Sorrow

She said she had been waiting for me, she stood in the finest of Bridal Gowns

So sweet was her Kiss that I immediately asked for her Hand

I came to love our Lady of the Harvest

We were Wed in the ruins of a long forgotten cemetery

There were cherry blossoms and grape vines all around us

The stars above us gave chorus to our Union

We joined and I told her words that had never before been spoken

I told her the riddle of my Heart---"What breaks without being touched and opens without a door?" and how it beats with the Life of the Ancient Sailor

Now I had finally found a Friend, Lover, and Companion in Sadness

In this Lives the Blood of Words

In this I have become One with Sweet Sadness

I believe I belong in Hell for my Crimes against God, yet I suspect he sees something in the Mirror of my Soul that I cannot

I only see a Monster consumed by its own Lust

I have become so lost in my own Pride that I have betrayed my own Desires

But admitting these faults has led me towards understanding them

For I've constructed my own Prison

My hatred for the Darkness that has Infected me knows no limits

Here on my Throne of Self-Destruction I torture myself beyond Regret

But the Pain I cause myself is a form of Purification

In the secret places of my Mind there is the smallest seed of the Divine

I long to Forgive my Enemies, I long to let go of my Anger

I try in my Heart to Love things beyond Pleasure, I long to Love for Love's Sake

I believe this to be the most Pure and Noble form of Love that can Exist

I believe God Loves us not because we are Good but because we are part of him

This is why I Love Sadness---for the Wisdom it engenders

I know my Sins sadden God, but when I in turn experience Great Sadness, I become therefore able to experience the Love inherent to Divine Sadness

I believe in Time my Soul's Sickness will be Cured by the Presence of God

This is why I embrace Sadness, it is as close to God as I can get

I can feel the Love that surrounds his Distant Kingdom, but I cannot reach it

This is my Sadness, but what a Noble thing it is, for it gives me the Knowledge of God's Existence

Visions

The darkness flows over me in shadows of fog, and embers burn away my memory and words---all seems lost

Only tombstones lie ahead of me, and the morbid riddle of fame offers no comfort

The love that imbues my words has been lost to time, and the wind that blows through the sands howls in an almost forgotten dream of all that I have spoken

I see myself crowned and robed in chains that are pulling me towards oblivion---a hole that has grown into an abyss inside of me

The darkness slowly inundates and surrounds me

I lose decades-worth of memories as I drown in my own past

How long will this haunted dream last? I've become undone

As they rip through my flesh, blackened wings emerge from my shoulders

Scars appear across my face as the wisdom that is born only of age transforms me into something mutated---an abomination

The thirst of excess calls me to its indulgence, making me a slave to its black-hearted wine of doubt and self-loathing

Anger pools within my eyes as I stare at the disfigured shell of my soul

Needles of pain shoot through my head as horns begin to grow out of my skull

I've become the monster of my own dread

Black nails emerge from my fingers and puncture my chest, enabling the dark entities that abide within me to pour out

The gates of Hell open within my thoughts, and shadowy figures dance about the flames that engulf my mind

These lightless flames ignite my body

The pain and stench of my searing flesh streak through my brain in a shrieking voice of murder and mayhem

Black eyes stare back at me from the mirror of my confession

Here lies the wellspring of hatred and loss

Empowered by self-pity, the ego seeks to satisfy its own lust for power and revenge

Now I am a dark angel who fights to resist his own wrath-obsessed nature with all that is still human within me

The darkness has come to consume my memory of light and hope, the threads of which I still cling to in a world of shadow and regret

All around me impaled bodies stretch across the horizon, creating a forest of the dead that imprisons me with their blank stares and rotting flesh

Is this the kingdom that I am to inherit---a throne of corpses and shameful regrets?

This vision of despair grasps and tears at whatever memories of good still remain within me, attempting to make me to forget

Murdered angels create a landscape of crucified heroes, some of which are burned to a cinder

I stumble and lurch through this dark dimension which is nothing but an endless land of death and misery, lead on only by fate, for my will has been subdued

I've become a shadowy apothecary to the dead who haunt my eyes and who cry for some glimpse at resurrection

In such hopelessness I have found it important to hold on to whatever fragments of light may still flicker in my memory

And as I walk down this road of emptiness, I pause to consider my purpose in this haunted kingdom of ghosts and dead angels

I will see to it that none of their lives were given in vain---today a dark angel of light has been born from shadow and flesh

The Blue Dark Light

A new voice of lost reason awakened me with the sobering sting of confusion

The helpless fragments of my soul crawl toward each other wishing to bind with this blue dark blinding light, as if the fire in my ancient heart had imploded into the fusion of a building nova

No more need for guns or anger, only the overpowering feeling of knowing that the truth briskly passing over my shoulder gives me a reason to be---a purpose to embrace gravity and let my weight multiply

As if the hand of God had waved fresh air into my bleeding lungs, the stone of my heart sinks deep into this new burning ocean

But there's no sense of drowning, for I can swim freely without the need for breathing

I've become a cure---a virus feeding off its own massing energy

There's a lost thought of sickness floating into the embers all around me

No more fear of life or death---no placement of emptiness, as if to taste the word of God on my tongue---only the orgasmic freedom from what I thought I needed

The face of my body is melting away into a sky of ghostly arms

My blood is seething with golden snowflake boils in the mortar of atoms exploding all around me

The consuming matter becomes something new

This giant ant mound falls beneath me turning into the smallest point of a needle

The ground has no use of holding together

It gives way to a chilling wind of waking dead roses

The thorns inject their seeds and grow faster than a wildfire in the light of my eyes

Destruction is put away---all alone it fades into the blue color's hue

The birth of a billion towers engulf what I assume was the horizon

It's difficult to tell up from down

My sense of being is too large to be held in the center of a galaxy

I swallow up black holes one by one while a growing knowledge of hunger builds within me

The planets are ripped apart all around me becoming one with this sphere of pure energy

Where did the light come from? It's beyond seeing

I've lost the desire of form---there's only enlargement

The thorns turn blue and their petals bleed the fabric of what I thought love, hate, right and wrong could become

The universe itself is bending under the pressure of joining this ball of matter

Silence comes to bare a word---oneness

If only my mind would shed its pride I could open the path to its end---to be free of its disbelief

I'm right at its gate pounding on the unturnable key

My confession comes slowly in order to not wake its sin any more

It lays sleeping in the bed of demon whores, with angel tears hovering over the bed of my lost virgin

Well enough I never found her, though, for all is taken from a person on a dark high road such as mine---this road of "freedom"

I dare not say, "redemption", not without finding the tower's end

I fashion my new sword in truth, my shield into righteousness

Give funeral to the weapons of knowing

Turn me back to the ways of old, lest I be surprised

I aim my bullets of heart like a lion-bard with a pen

Guide them true to the one who tried to teach me the song of hate, God willing, if I'm at all sure

Give cry to the cross that gives pardon, for I still wish to bare its son's pain, as proof that I would still give him payment for what the Father and Son freely offered me on their table

I'm gripped by my desire's weight and the ones who would spite man, for they filled my plate with sin

So I owe a debt

For generations they hoped to break the cycle, yet I would stoop to complete it---I would carry this and more

Still I must ask if I have the right to kill, or must I simply construct a chain of justice?

Regardless of fate's will, in the end I'll pursue not as a god, but as a man on a quest for payment of souls and worlds destroyed

Coming in the darkness are the ones sent by the darkness to hinder my way, or worse still, to stray me from the narrow path

Allow me a horse of enlightenment that I may not stray!

Let my few friends six feet deep see me ride towards fate, so as to warn me of my actions

Who could dare? I say there are some, but few---so let the few become as one

I was riding across the desert, following the blood of death, when my thoughts surrendered to the idea that I couldn't be the only one of the world's dead or the ones dying that must give chase

Let us unite, I say! Let us follow the trail, lest we become it!

The spirit finally spoke after what seemed an eternity

It let man again join the game of chess, for new pawns were needed

So the fathers of old wept, for they could only watch from the windows of old death

As their sons met their fate in search of the one God whom none could find whilst still living

Yet I hadn't started in search of him til late in my birth

I had started to learn first from hate, yet I saw its end before it consumed me

Hate can claim your enemies, but with none left for it to consume, it must feed on the ones for whom it serves

This is where I witnessed the first light of truth

So I sought peace, but instead found only a new nightmare

When I woke from my first slumber, the horror of this world showed its need for war

I met it with words but would end it with my last possible breath in this world

Yet death would provide no rest for me---I would move from chess board to chess board and world to world in search of those who had taught us war, wishing only to right the wrongs in this time allowed to me

Why should a pawn become anything else?

It would only serve one king

When it can serve a world of kings, that my friend, becomes a winning strategy

Therein lies the truth of pawns---to never take a place of stature or pride

Only peace gives the knight rest

So I follow my old friends War and Death where I must

When peace breaks the sky I move to the next space of war

Til all wars end I'll find no home

I indenture myself to the God of kings---send me where thou wilt

I'm the stone that will not be lifted

There are so many false gods still left to fight

Why should I let death persuade me to die?

With all of these dark angels following me and calling my name, I'll become nameless in this house of shame

When I find those who doubt the light and take the hand of darkness, I will then be pulled to the hand of judgment

I must answer their voiced cries, yet with my own hands I can't wash away the blood of the damned

Who is innocent? Not I

I escaped the fire by fate and by the will of a Ghost

All too well I've learned the secrets of my enemies, having therefore been left to battle the temptation to so easily become one of them

Help me to escape this monster---this song of war!

My only request is for but a few hours of peaceful slumber away from the nightmare of fiery horses

I pray at some point you will finally let me know the unknown song of worlds at peace!

The Madness it Takes to Evolve

It's a sad commentary to realize that suicide would offer me no comfort at all

There's no greater sense of "being lost" than that which accompanies the soul that's deprived of slumber

No need for dreams of peace, there remain only thoughts of revelation

We're overcome and worlds apart from the insights forgotten by so-called civilization

No hope in darkness, save a candle's flicker that barely provides a glow

This infinite light could truly show us how our lifetimes come to pass

In the end, they're but memories of a reality that couldn't last

For too long it's seemed pointless for me to live or die anymore

I still drift in and out between worlds and my corpse's tongue still speaks from the halls of an unkempt tomb

The wolves still gather at the remaining steps

They offer song at the ruins of the temple of what's beyond the forgotten door

I'm darkness and light---I'm the afterbirth of second sight---I'm wrath born of anger

Awakened and disturbed by heaven's outcast, I've been revived to consume the sun

I helplessly watch the world come undone

I've come to silence the beggars of emotion's starved sons

I've come from the grave to sing to the unsung

Death is my anthem---chaos is my crown

I can't escape from the darkness that's pulling me down

I've become a nightmare within a nightmare---I've stepped into oblivion

The mask I present is only an illusion of beauty

This monster who stands before you is the result of your own handiwork

So jump into the abyss---I'm sure you won't be missed

Go ahead and kill me---all I want is for you to know the pain that fallen angels feel

Your horrors are all I've known of life

Now it's your turn to come and embrace the chains of strife

Madness Seems Needed

The slow siege of pain and isolation that's brought on by longing and loneliness

The forsaken feeling of fear turning to anger

The desire for my suffering to be shared en mass

The will of the mind to rationalize the purity of inflicting one's own pain upon others

It seems the only chance for a moment of freedom

I see the darkness growing and infecting my soul like a virus

The only way to soften its wrath is to spread its gloom

I'm becoming a servant to my tormentors---I'm becoming a monster

My soul seems jaded and cross---I'm losing the capacity for mercy

Yet some part of my mind's eye keeps me from releasing the spirits of doom

I must torment myself to keep my tormentors at bay

I shriek out a prayer in hopes of keeping myself imprisoned behind the fortress of my mind

I can only hope that anyone else who happens to suffer from this same madness could understand the need for self-affliction

Ah, the beautiful anguish of restraint!

There are so many lies out here

They would claim me a god---an unremorseful, unrelenting machine set out on a course of genocide

A ruler of ruin and isolation, yet I choose to suffer that which I would impose on the guilty

The entire time my soul hungers for the long-forgotten skies of bliss

I'm but a ghost swept away in the wind of a cold starless night

A sense of belonging is forever lost

Now there's only the endless solitude of the highway

The highway man staggers forward through the gates of hell

Lost in the world of fallen Eden, heaven seems but a misplaced memory scattered from the moment of now

There's only one name that lights the embers of the blue rose and only one place where I remember the humanity of feeling

The Hanged Man

The hanged man forever dancing in the gallows with one last trick up his sleeve, another card to play

Here in shadows of past and future I call out to the dead

In ancient prayer they beckon me to ride forth with them because sometimes the dead do not rest

So I ride forth with famine and war, another pale rider with hell following close behind me

I hold the scales of worth for the blind lady of justice

Please welcome me in your embrace for I am weary from my travels

Beyond the damp darkness stare empty souls

With hopeless eyes the complacent grow in number as their world slowly crumbles to ash

Who will wake them from their lost red, white, and blue dreams of yesterday?

The flames of freedom die down as the flag of compromise is raised over the land

History repeats itself over again, and over time the ultimate loss becomes well within reach

But now may the waters be cleansed

I am weighed down and pulled to the bottom

Standing at the brink of civilization on a lowly road, my feelings are empty as I view the sky and its mocking clouds

How can I escape this nothingness?

But it was in fields of amber and gray that I gained courage from the dark shadows of existence

Knowledge has poisoned me in my mind's eye with the acknowledgement of my own insignificance

How useless it all seems now given its tremendous scale

We all seek a purpose and I'm still searching for my own within these lacey words of continuous thought

In cold blood and violent color do I see the blue dreams of my bliss

Faded, dusty, almost forgotten, but still burning a candle of old-fashioned hope

Memories search the streets of yesterday with longing as they flood my soul with brief moments of life once again

Who could wake me from my crypt in this graveyard of awareness?

Long have I pondered these questions in the meadows of the afterlife

Long enough to carry its stones from the eyes of my youth

Heavy is my conscience as it burdens me with the after-sight of my years

Here there is no warm hand to embrace, only the cold of night and its eternal moon of pale glow

But the weight of it all increases through my inactivity

They are forcing me to take a stand for the sake of the infinite light

Should I rise from this dead world?

Can the animal within be hindered from its chase by dawn's birth on new shores?

Desire causes a hunger that can pull one from a high peak of impartial observation to a fatal state of primitive pleasure

In whirlpools of lust and vice, excess is a sad place of wisdom where the lessons cannot be unlearnt

I have learned that the weight of one's actions is measured by the stones of the heart

But although hell is definitely deserved, I have high hopes for my rescue

But will I die before I get it right?

Who can slay the unrestrained appetite of neediness that destroys all?

For now I cast away all that I have treasured from my conquests in love and war

I am part of the darkness of secret hope, where it meets the light in balanced chords

For there cannot be one without the other

The serpent of my tongue slithers in the forbidden garden of knowledge where age's price ends in repetition (alas, more stones to carry)

That serpent of old has told me many tales under the ancient tower of shadow and light

But now I long for release, for I am a son of war

For it was in war that I was born and it will be in war that I shall die

Song of the Hanged Man

So now I end my pursuit of death and pursue life as a friend and not as a lover

Oh how high these deserts have lifted me---take me old raven to the sky

Let me know the stars of the present as my light

For who can call the future but the sun?

I've tasted life's fruit and thank the earth mother

I thank the universe for this infinity of lives through the sadness and through the joy

Now is the time to honor the father and maker

I call upon the moon in her tide of storms through the dead of night

I set sail, though unsure of what the ship promises

Take me beyond this mortal love of what is to be

And let the tragedy of my story bring glory to the tempest of my divine joy

For I've tasted every treasure upon this dance of words

And music guides my spirit of old to the cloud of wisdom

For its delight is upon my tongue

Thus, I'm eternally grateful to have truly lived

The Gates of the Crypt

I feel the tides of gravity, the obsessed hands of broken fate

The swaying, brushing wings in the candle's storm of long-closed, tomb-borne gates

Let me walk among the somber in that darkness, ever-crossing the unknown bridge among the sands that have into the witching hours called and fallen forever late

I'm the keeper of the ruin, the tongue-chained, hopelessly bound to the bitterness of the forbidden embers given by the cruel emotions of what is an eternal waiting

Set firm my footprints upon the brimstone leading past the shores of emptiness

I walk headlong into oblivion, comprehending awareness in dreams without slumber

Upon my gaze are impaled angels embedded in their fathomless number

They mark a path with eyes forever staring into the horror of their final woe

This is where I leave my last years of regret and step forward onto the crossroads beyond where mortal soul is to ascend

I've seen too much to go back to the world of the living, yet I'm also unable to find reason among the dead

I am a highway man, forever drifting in between worlds and words that still remain unsaid

Beyond long, I cross the valley of death into the desert of the damned

I go forward onto the unseen suffering of haunted chamber beds

The highway man sails on, sailing toward the desires that remain still unfed

Highway Man's Song

I speak in riddles, I speak in codes

I am the highway man of the empty road

I dance with angels, I dance with devils

In the midnight hour I sing with rebels

Oh dear lord won't you take me home?

I've been gone so long, could you take me home?

Out here it remains unclear, this sense of loss and taste of fear

This endless blacktop of souls and truck stops

And the hanged man dances on the gallows singing, "Oh lord did I really do it all so wrong?"

I've been gone so long, could you take me home?

Take me to the seven candles highway

The Song of the Wolf

The undead poet rises---long have I slept

The song of the wolf has come and awakened me

Here, past the riddle of fame, ego, and pride, I've searched the multiverses

In humble tears I embrace the truth of suffering

It has brought much thought and terrible wisdom of the transgressor called man

From my watchtower of exile I've observed as creation has become perverted

Here in the garden of memories we all may recall the fair skies of Eden

We've wandered far from the mother of creation

Can none recall her trees of shelter and the sweet fruit of her wine?

The ghost-dance calls to me there

I shall not forget my father's face or the songs of his maker who gave him birth from clay

Lifetimes fall upon lifetimes---death and birth become one

All that is holy is knowledge and enlightenment

Revelations fall like rain upon my face

Come, oh dreams of red, white, and blue---be nightmares no more

Who will give cry for our forgotten mother?

From my tower of exile I release the wolves of my throne upon the world, for the song of the wolf has come

The dark forest calls to me and I've given ear to the words of her song

For too long has the world forgotten the songs of life, thus now comes the sweet charms of death

Smoke fills the sky and we thus die a little more with each breath

I call to lost Eden and the tree of life to deliver the blood of words in order to warn us of what we've lost and have cast aside

And now come the pains of the earth and sky to rain down upon us

Who shall rise to save the garden?

Or shall I call upon the pale horse to read you your fortune?

I call upon the dark star, I call upon the dark moon, I call upon the dark mask, I call upon the light

Come, oh fire of forges, give surrender to the magnetar, ride through the black holes of time and turn them into infinite light

Spheres of pure mass and boundless energy call out, my soul's blood boils in the colliding snowflakes of comets and dead planets

Bury me in the weight of a trillion suns, fragment my bones to the edges of the universe

Let me taste the abyss of oblivion and beyond, to the fabric of being I pledge my sacrament to the lighthouse of the lost

Let the thunder of my words guide you to its light---out into the void of emptiness and unmaking

I howl into the face of sadness to the bottom of her black heart, to rise once more as her forgotten son

Unto the song of the wolf I bend my chords, and to the moon I bind my heart

May God find his rest in me, let my wandering eyes be blinded so that I may better hear the wisdom of mystery

Oh come curse, curse of infinite tears, hear oh immortal lifetimes, my death of a thousand swords

For you have created a monster of hate and lost love and I beg let me not murder the memory of light, let it ever haunt me

From here I enter the eyes of the wolf and he drinks from the cup of stars

Stretched in his ghost, my face melts away into the fog of the present

Time folds in on itself, bending reality, and I capture vague glimpses of the future before they flash into the unknown

I rise from death and hell as a new creation, but not before coming face-to-face with my horrible adversary

I call upon the magnetar in howls of pain and delightful abandon

Blind me so that I may stand upon the shores of your birth song, that I may be found worthy of true enlightened thought

Clear my mind of the illusion of this world and let me see the multiverses

Alas, let the wolves of time run free and immortal in the face of the light

Let us serve the light and bring an end to the endless night

Howl, oh great wolf of lost time, and hear, tear the flesh of this earth with your fires and let your tears become oceans of sand

Let me know the thirst of your heart---call the white raven

For the time has come to face him for one last dance at the gallows of the hanged man of Golgotha

The Time to Stand

Oh how far I've fallen in this world of slow decay from nightmares of darkness and self-loathing

I've returned to love myself and create worlds of beauty from the ashes of my horror

I walk forward in the face of doubt to face the countless fears I ran from for centuries

Here in the twilight of experience I'll make my stand

For death has been my mistress, but life is my eternal love

I've returned to wake the dead and dance in long-forgotten cemeteries

I call out to the God of old with my ancient song, to bring the light of existence to a shadowed world

I offer my blood as the ink of my words and my flesh as the pages of my book

I present them to the fire of eternity

Let there be wisdom given to the loveless, and to the wicked, make them face the wisdom of truth

The Kingdom of Stars

I sit upon my throne of fire and wonder

Stars rest at my feet, for my kingdom is far from this world

I've returned from the hollows of endless night to seek but a loving voice in this ocean of silence

Long have I stood singing to the cosmos, hearing only my echo

The shadows of nightmares and dreams blend into my very soul, yet I continue walking in flames of glory, for the nova of my heart is building into an unstoppable force of energy and mass

The suns rays bend at my call and the moon bares my sadness in tides of tempest storms of want and thirst that are legendary, even in hell

Death seems but a faded memory, for God refuses to let me die or even rest until I return this love that burns eternally within me

Who is worthy to look upon the horrors of my heart?

Scars of endless arrows rest upon my chest like medals from a long-forgotten battle

For lifetimes I've felt no gentle hand or even the touch of the living, yet I'm still building light and strength

There seems to be no limit to what I could do to the universe, yet my curse is to be alone, for such power seems to come at a cost

The will of my mind screams---pulling at the fusion of a trillion suns within me

Black holes turn in fear of the everlasting light of my creation

But I can tell no one of my victory over the tree of the knowledge of good and evil

Who can share my wisdom of enlightenments in this lost city of abandon (for my throne is far from the kingdoms of men)?

But know that I'm growing---know that I'm gaining mass

Behold, the birth of the Magnetar

Prayers of Tears

The great emptiness of sadness calls out to me from beyond the veil

I offer my joy unto the sacrifice of the blue flame and to the mystery of what is to come

To my daughter, give her bliss in exchange for my lament

Let her roam free in the lost garden

Give her the blue rose of my eternal love

I've already tasted paradise and I've survived the cold ice of unmet desires for this long, so I therefore wait in my tower of exile for my time of ascension into the starry kingdom

Let her song be heard and allow her to dream of endless possibilities

Give her the truth and peace she seeks

Let her thoughts take flight into clouds of enlightened wisdom

May her family live eternally under the tree of life

In this voyage of life, give her the treasures of the heart and let her candle burn forever in the light

Dark Confession

My dark confession haunts my crowded soul and I've died a thousand times over

I search onward for truth and redemption in the face of a suffering that was experienced on a divine level---for the utter darkness was proof of the light

I shall neither kneel to time nor death, for my quest is eternal, and the God I serve is worthy of his glory

The wisdom of the earth and trees fills me, and I feel her pangs

I call to the stars and the song of the wolf to bring back the blood moon of old so that man may remember the words of life and cast aside his love for death

Some knowledge belongs only to poets and prophets and isn't intended for crowns and kings---so that they may frivolously assert their influence

Thus I call to you to return in humility to our noble mother and to honor her ways

The alternative is to take one more step closer to oblivion and to stare with eyes wide open into the horrors from which I've scarcely returned

And I bid you heed this warning---the undead poet lives

To the Dark Magicians

The dark songs lay siege to blackened minstrels and temples of shadows

The lament of eons gives wailing background chorus to cold winds dancing in the flames of forever night

Hold fast the reigns of nightmare steeds and dreams lost to time

Here shine the keys of my lost moral and its wealth of wisdom

The thirst of centuries is upon my tongue

The hand of age crushes my bones with its mixture of earth and fire

Resurrect my repentance from ash and pit

Let me see through the ghost of my eyes

Let me walk through the galaxies of this universe and its creation

Give feast to the hunger of divinity---alas, let the temple be cleansed by the expulsion of my blood

Take the grave of my heart into the furnace of forging

I will atone for my sins of the flesh and for my wanton desire

Give court to the ancient legend and to all of the entities stretched out through the sands of existence who've spoken to me beyond the vail of melody and melancholy

Here upon the edge of the abyssal plains and in the labyrinth of the void of eternity, I've come to understand the balance of sadness and joy that accompanies the mystery of the birth of man

I ask to what end and what purpose do we dance---for good or for evil?

The Phantom of Song

For what is to be, I call upon the sun and moon

I sing to the wolves of my heart and the love therein

Hear, oh bride of the infinite night, for my unchained desires burn with the truth of my worth

Drink from the wine of my tears and know that there is none sweeter

Taste the blood of my countless lifetimes and the glory of my throne

For I'm the phantom of song, and I can take your heart or soul with but a word from song of lament, for I've sailed through oceans of hate and love

What face could draw me, the phantom of song, from my throne of exile?

Is there still a soul pure enough to tame the wolves of my heart and melt my tears of ice?

Oh love of ancient tides, sing your song to me, call upon the night with your moon and bring the son of song your gentle caress

Let me know the ghost of your touch and the longing of your wistful eye

I've returned from countless tombstones to hear your voice and to breathe upon your neck the perfume of life once more

I've come to find the waters of soft words in the locks of your hair

I dream of the fire in your eyes and the echo of your joyful dance

Join me in my dark tower of ghostly hymns

From angels of timeless harmony I call upon the stars to bring me my unforgotten bride

For I long to rest in your bosom and hear the beat of your virgin heart

I've crossed a bridge of infinite darkness to stand in your graceful light

For your name is the song of my tongue and I shan't slumber until you know my face again and free me from these chains of endless desire

Your memory calls to me beyond these shores of longing and I've come to find your hand and to make it mine at last

For true love is an eternal waltz

The Monster of Love

Dead souls and afterbirth---the slow decay of black flowers

I stumble through the gravestones of lost loves and stand upon the truth of wisdom

The love I seek has been within me all along

My eyes are engulfed by the infinite moon and her song so divine

Her voice makes such music that I've never been alone, for the night walks with me always

I'm the angel of sadness, devourer of the hearts and souls of those who dare to cast my love away

I live in the shadow of grace with such desires that even make the devil weep

Come to the valley of the rose and taste my words, for the love I hold is true, but its hunger is endless

To enter my tower of exile you must be pure and hold the blue flame of sanctuary, for the consuming nature of my love tests the heart

Come ye witches, demons, and devils and I shall reap your hearts from your very chests as they yet beat, for I'm the monster of love, and even death holds no sway over me

I'm eternal, for true love is forever---from lifetime to lifetime

I grow anew from womb to birth to grave

I dance in sweet gloom with the ghost of my love

Risen from the Grave

I rise from the grave in resurrection, led by a hand that emerges from the dark forest

Upon the winds I whisper to the secret gardens, "I've not forgotten what we've lost"

For I can no longer stand by and watch you tear it down, this holy mother that fed me with her tears and shaded me with her trees

Transgression burns the sanctuary

The freedom of life has its sacred chamber

Ghost-dance in her pale moonlight, my forgotten brothers of the plains, for the law of the land has soured in the hands of this creation that's called "man"

You've forgotten your pact with the earth

She rises in tempest storms and earthquakes, all the while moaning in travail in response to our bloody deeds

Blackbirds fly in dawns of children lost to time

The Burning Forest

Trees seeping in birth pangs in fires of the netherworld---the flames rise in a horror of smoke and ash

Here in the sacred forest opens the mouth of abomination

The trees cry out in ancient prayer---oh how sad it is this flame that engulfs the canopy

A river of tears storms from the eyes of the natives, they're as ghosts haunting the soul

I can feel misshapen figures dance amongst the flames

Here burn the fruits of Eden and the lost sons of Adam

From ancient times they cry out from within my soul

I'm set ablaze in the garden of this nightmare called reality

Man has dared to set the world on fire

How long would he ravage this earth and her children?

Lost Eden

What a great sorrow it is to realize both all that man has lost and all that he could have been

And what a humbling experience it is to stand amidst the horrible beauty of that loss

Can we find the keys to the kingdom again?

I say, "Yes", for through oceans of sadness in sublime sorrow I have yet to be drowned because I've grown strong

I've swum through the darkness and been reborn as a blue-thorned rose in the garden of memories

Standing alone here, my petals open in the darkest of night where midnight calls the moon and stars to enjoy infinite leisure

I open my heart to the ghosts of the hour and their spirits pour through me so as to feel the mortal pleasure of life once more

Some are angelic ascending spirits and some are demons---some are so ancient that they're lost to time

I stand alone in their sad embrace for I, too, have known the pain of a lost life

I feel the joy of the dance as I lose myself in the midnight chords of sorrow

I turn to a friend---a place where my tower of exile shines in the dreams of possibilities

Having returned from the "shadow of death", I now find joy in the smallest of experiences

My life of excess has left me caught in between the doors of life and death

Thus I've learned the value that every living creature holds

I give song to the nightbird and to the damned who are lost in endless night

Within cemeteries so secret I dance with the dead in the shining moonlight, all the while bathed in stars from the strangest of skies

Who among you knows how the taste of darkness can become like the comforting greeting of a friend?

In the arms of death we dance together in sweet loneliness

In ghost songs of lives gone by would you dare to cross the great void of madness to reach the far shores of lost Eden?

For under the tree of life will I make my bed and there will I dream of a heaven not lost to time

From my own hell I've risen through the deepest depths of the galaxy and have now come to smile down upon the multiverse in weeping laughter and in celebration of the triumph of the soul and will

From my own hell I awake and repent and dream of lost Eden

Let me slumber with the animals and enjoy the friendship of creation

Let me dance and howl at the moon in jungles of unspoiled purity

The wolves of my heart will howl in naked delight as I run through the forest without shame with the animals

In great song and dance will I sing to the joy of the moon

The moon's dark forest opens upon shores uncharted

I'm the ghostbird singing with ravens and black wings

Oh woe unto lost Eden and these black and blue thorns of both horror and beauty whose petals glow with the bluest roses of all that was lost

It's forever dreamed of but never obtained by the fog of dawn, this unforgettable lost Eden

Now I stand in the shadow of oblivion and darkness to hold the candle of blue flame

Through nightmares beyond dreams I've seen the face of repugnancy that's caught in its pride and arrogance

Where are the dreams we were promised by the infinite moon?

In days gone by, we celebrated our glory in years that passed all-too-soon

I cry out with a great hole in my heart as I'm simultaneously held in the arms of life and death

If only I could dance once more in the wedding ceremony that transcends death and gloom

By what ego do I have the right to sing of melancholy?

By the right of all I've lost in the face of poor lost Eden, I say

Give me strength once more, oh "enchanted forest", for I've not forgotten your promised bliss

Here in the darkest depths of the soul I shed a tear for all that lives---and woe unto lost Eden

Looking for a New World

I call upon the Gods to hear my noble plea

I pray for their birth upon mortal shores

For within them I've looked through the eyes of death and found myself waiting for their return

Let them return us to the paths of the sublime

In the loneliness of mortality I left the security of land to sail the seas of adventure

Let me be lost to the tide so I may be born again in their true image

Alas, let me find a new world

Blue

Here in the lonely echoes of the cold winds I remember the comforting chill of rain

The open hands of time fall in tears upon your broken wings when I say your name

Calling like a tempest, born to wed the storm, I climb the exile of desire upon the mountains where I see your color touch the waters

I can taste love in the shadows of your cruel fire

Blue and black are the oceans of my symbols there

I feel my soul start to tremble

Was it all just a jaded dream? Is this the burden of a silent scream?

I remember you---I'm still in love with the roses that you turned to blue

You turned me into that blue

I offer up my flesh in accordance with the subtle seduction

Falling from the charms of dissolution and over-reached beyond the fate of kings, I taste bloody purity as it trickles down the crowns of doubting pleasures

I found the truth in lament, inside this maddening overcast that has shown me the blinding torment of unmet fulfillment

I'm beyond your subtle burdens of seductions

At last, I'm greeted by the fruits of divine contemplation

I leap to the horse of nightmares and charge headlong into the face of God's forgotten path of clarity

Here in dark chambers, I hold the embers of your tainted gifts and I cherish their blue glow of what has been lost

I journey into the gates of the damned searching for the ghost of our joining

Deeper into my crypt, I shall shriek out tones of lingering loneliness til the winds themselves storm into echoes legendary, even in hell

For even the devil himself will stand in disbelief at the earthquakes that will be created by the spirits within me

Shaking his foundations, he will stare speechless in astonishment as the walls of his kingdom shutter from my wails

I haunt your memories, still dancing above the coffin of our shared moments

Even death cries tears of blue diamonds, for she can see the groaning chains of tormented spirits in eternal moan that travel the labyrinth of a stone that was once a heart

In my self-imposed prison I grasp at what was stolen, and I shall hold what was once the blue

I and the spirits within me shall search the universe and beyond, forever restless til your eyes finally gaze upon my true glory---a falling angel of blue's deepest hue

Immortal Love

As an old vampire, I long for my lost humanity

For my love has been taken by the hands of time

Shall I long for her in our lost cemetery and lament upon her tombstone?

Shall I punish the world of the living for going on without her?

Even in death I've found my way back to her

I dance in ghostly charm upon nights where the moon shines bright, and hold her close to my heart

Most would call me dark and devilish, but what do they know of true immortal love?

I've crossed every bridge in memorial to her love

In desperate hours, the ways of the heart are dark indeed

I've dared walk "where angels fear to tread" to continue our love affair beyond death's cruel grasp

Oh how my crowded soul longs to rest in your arms my cryptic bride

Let me bring you the blue rose of timeless love

I shall make the world remember your tears by burning their kingdoms to the ground

Birthing Monsters

Demons of lust impose upon my isolation

With all of my strength I battle their onslaught

Lonely and full of horrors is the road of truth

I longed to be fitted with a mask in order to hide the monster within

But that time has passed, let the world look on in terror at the creature they've made

In my abandon, I long for blood and revenge

Yet I see past these fantasies, on to a world of my own

A place where I've stacked every brick in my tower of exile

The sounds of music come to hold me and remind me of my task

In order to stand in the fires of love, I must place my heart in its forge

Alas, let it give birth to a new monster of light and allow me to love alone

Shadows of Night and Memory

All hail the shadows of night and the embers of memory!

I stand alone in their ashes---the fire within my soul still burns, never surrendering to the dark voids of my inner mind

In my bones the blood still flows through rivers of unshed tears

I walk on through the lonely desert of my conscience and carry the torch of my lost desire

Coming closer to the stars I smile at the silent moon that lights my way

Her wisdom guides me on, alone I hear her endless song coming ever closer with the answers of immortality

I go beyond this life and I forsake the hand of death in my black cloak of grayed years

Refusing to die by my own hand, as this world had wished, and now I challenge the false teachings of the tin gods, and I dare to make my sacrifice to the noble cause that remains beyond the self

Into the roads of lost legends I make my way by will and force of mind

Engaging the pains I once ran from to learn from the tragedy of my mistakes

My pen is sharpened into a sword by casting away the ego I once wore so proudly

I want to become the nameless one as I invite the spirits to take their rightful place within me to share this life beyond the fears of men with all who have lost theirs for our cause

We grow in number by taking the hard road of long toil to serve a purpose beyond what the eyes can see

Who will join us and shed their blood for truth and true freedom of mind and soul?

I carry only words and knowledge for weapons, and their power is greater than steel

Pick them up and carry them to find your comfort, for I've found something beyond this reality

Do I stand alone on the mountain of inner pleasure?

I think not, because there's something guiding me on when I tire of these mortal restraints

Hard was the recklessness of my youth, but I've outgrown its usefulness

In my heart I see the face of my father---his voice tells me to journey on, so I do

When all hope is lost and life seems to have no true purpose, I carry the flag for the ghosts of all our ancestors and the lives they gave

What is it you live for, if not them?

Find a cause to believe in once more

What is it you're willing to fight for, if not this?

I'm willing to die for what I believe, thus I will live forever

Ode to Death

Ode to death, old sweet friend---long feared, but now realization calls me to your sweet caress

To dance in the arms of my promised bride, where I'll forget my name and the horrors that are associated with it

Let loose morbid dreams of murder and revenge

Let their blood fall silent to the ground in these nightmares of my life and its transgressions

For hell's upon me---I've wandered far from the light into a darkness that gives fire to my mind's heartless abyss

There's a desire to kill without judgment, driven by the need to destroy life, to cleanse the earth in a graveyard of impaled bodies, til their corpses become a forest of the dead

"Leave no stone unturned", the spirits cried, as I slaughtered mother, daughter, son, and father, so as to become the very hand of death itself

And now I long for her to take me---for my bloodstained hands can't be cleansed

In this, my kingdom of hell, furnished with scorched earth and divine guilt, I long for release into the slumber of heaven

Alas, let my debt be paid---come death, destroyer of worlds---take me as repayment for the guilt of man

Knowledge's price seems too high---alas, let ignorance find its bliss

Free us from that fruit we partook of

I've wronged the mother of creation, thus I'm ready to pay my dark debt

I've seen the eyes of youth lost to the mirror

Strike down my ignorance and my belligerent mind in the darings of youth

In my folly I've died a thousand times

Must I accept devils as angels to escape my horrors---trading bliss for sorrow in a final act of shame?

What I know must be let loose and forgotten, for the dreams of crowns and kings are too highly treasured to be carried by the sons of man

Thus for whom do I write?

I write for the wise and the fool

I write for the madness that compels me and the spirits that haunt me

I write for the sorrow that I love to hate and that I hate to love

I write for lessons hard-learned

Alas, let all be forgotten into these faded dreams of the pale forest

The Gray Rider

The ancient souls and songs of the past chant in my thoughts, as if from some former life they had called to me

I'm the gray rider standing on the great plateau of the horizon

I look down upon a troubled world that's lost in glamour, greed, and illusion

I walk out upon a strange, cursed land, stolen in blood and murder

Souls pour out of the ripples in its flag, yet its people have forgotten the dead souls this has taken in its afterbirth

I cannot forget, for their blood floods the temple of my salvation

The dead are due their sacrament, so I wait among them to find slumber and birth in a new light

The dark angels come to give birth to the just rewards of the wicked

Here in my own shadow of excess I wait for my own day of judgment, thus the flag we wave is soaked in blood and the pearls of swine

Let us carry a new banner of spirit and thought into the infinite stars

I ponder how many lives we've lived and given our blood for

It's the gift of the unknown and I'll serve it forever

For wisdom's value far outshines the treasures of the flesh

Thus let me find myself joined with my friends of the sky in the great wisdom of the stars

Let me take my place beside them if I'm found worthy, for the restless spirits have made me weary

Still there are many miles to go before I cross that bridge that seems to have no end

I must stand naked before this world that has forgotten the ancient law and embrace its gifts

I look on to a new world through fire and ash and I walk into their consumption through life after life in world after world

Death consumes, but its tears give birth

The hanged man may yet live

My crypt is unkempt and there are no roses left to bloom upon my path

Through horror beyond the terror of madness I spread my wings to fly, for I'm driven, nay, compelled, to seek the light within the darkness

I'm a slave of truth, thus I must confess my unworthiness and find its redemption

Though it may destroy me, I must find a way to chain my desires

For some of them in the darkness of my soul abound, thus they belong dead

Sublime Dreams Creeping In

I gave way to slumber---in my weary state I passed over into the skies of painless clouds hoping dreams would take me to a lost garden

I found the throne-room taken by trees and rivers of wine

How had I stumbled into this enchanted kingdom of the unknown?

I had escaped from the banks of clarity

The flowers tasted of opium blooms

I was caught between dreams and petals that removed the gloom from reality

Let me sail to the shores of friendly moments

I can still see the ghostly shapes of lost lovers waving to each other from their exile of faded memories

Let me plot a course through the fog of their loss---for I wish to join them

Let me join the ghost dancers of past earthly graces

Maybe we can awaken the purple robes of wedding embers lifted high in the floating ashes of spent desires

Let us give song to our brother-moon and a toast to those young lovers who have yet to see the sparkling glowing gleam in the eyes of what they long for

Let it meet them in blue moonbeams and let all souls know the heart of truth---for truth is distant

It lingers in the stars, and for some it graces the tongue when it's welcomed

I'm just a new creature in this savage forest

Born to the wolves and their song that I shall soon succumb to

I'm also ready to take wing and join in with the ravens---bounding all around me, they long for me to sing with them their solemn song

Alas, here there are no troubled sonnets of remorse

So I shall take ear to these streams of the bouquet, far from the echoes of another world's war

Here hunger is unheard of and the act of lovemaking is but a thought sent by the kiss of imagination

Oh hear the cry of Eden!

In this place I wander the catacombs free from the tempting pleasures of the flesh---yet the perfumes of opium blooms seduce me

I find it more and more difficult to see the distant world below

I long to taste the sap of my comfort here

I gladly wear the crown of what some would call my despair

So let the world bleed me to prove I still walk among them

I'm reaching out across the chaos beyond the void---I'm casting my own pain adrift---I wish to go further

I would dare to grasp at the infinite---I search for truth and knowledge

I would dare to put my hand forward to know the suffering of God---I long to share his tears

I can feel the fringes of his pain, but I'm only a mortal, so how could I bare the full burden of his wounds?

A Strange Dream

In the late creeping of the moon, in its midnight hour, when others slumbered, I was awakened in a half sleep by a mysterious toning of bells

I gave chase for the charmed echoes tone---it compelled me forward into a shadowy mist

I followed the bells haunting tone into a place between day and night

There I could hear the laughter of children and the sublime ringing of those same bells

From where I knew not---the echoes grew until it became deafening

Grains of sand began to rain down upon me---I was being buried alive, but very slowly

All the grains represented my many lifetimes---they showered me with memories of both joy and sadness, bliss and tragedy

They crossed oceans and deserts, worlds and universes, for I've lived many times and I've had many names

I'm the shadow in the light---I'm the thunder in the rain---I'm what is but isn't seen

I'm a living ghost---I'm the warmth of the sunrise---I'm the dark of night, for I've lived many lives

The ringing bells wouldn't be silenced and the grains of sand seemed infinite

I was in an hourglass, held in place by sand and bottle

I watched the sands dance upon me as we ever-waited for the master who put us there to return

Come and wake me once more to turn my hands free, for I'm time itself, and I can be swayed by no man

Dead Dream

Dead thoughts in spoken whispers, slowly sifting through the ashes and the embers

There's nothing left to break, but inside I still remember

When does the candle's flaming wick wake the shadow's gleamer?

As fires smolder in stillborn desires, the helpless emotions crumble

Finally decaying into the sunset of a thunder's rumble

Yes, I've been haunting this game for so long and I'm still stuck in the remnants of a eulogy song

Now I clearly see the justice of my desolation

Yes---let me taste the wine of astonishment's crown

Let my repentance find preservation

Let the tongue of mercy shoulder us all

Faded Seasons

October nights fade from September skies, bleeding into cold December and January flights

I burn the candles to remember the green fires that lived inside your hazel eyes

Crossed and somewhat jaded, the dreams seem to refuse to die

I watch them explode into the brightest lights of dying suns

I wake up and join them because I know I'll soon become one

Yeah, sometimes I shine too bright just trying to escape the loss during the cold and lonely nights

So let my lantern shine

I live in a clock I can't rewind, but still I try to stop the hands that imprison time

So let the nova of the stars be my sign

Tear open the soft skies---there's no reason to ask them why

Kill me softly for all the intoxicants I've tried

Let me off the elevator so I can step into the sun

I'm tired of playing the rabbit in the moon

Simply allow me to shine for the suffering ones

Heart in a Cage

I took my heart from its stage

I traded the light for their darkest cage

My ego swelled my tongue, then time burned the page

I'm standing in a moment that's beyond age

It's priceless, the laughter we find in forever passing over a slumber of tombs in an outlived phase

I stand before my kingdom---I see the ranks filled with sedated idealists staring with empty gaze

Who will wave the banner to awaken an army?

Who will stand before me to awaken the world?

I shout to the heavens from a nightmare's prison

Into the spiral my life is hurled

Falling isn't an option---escape is but a dream

They silence the answers and ignore a universe of screams

Injuries and viruses have taken their toll

Astonished and bewildered, my eyes grow old

Warfare is all that's left of a cross made of peace

Plague and damnation roll like waves on a beach

The battle is tided by ghosts locked in a stalemate

The world fills with blindness---perhaps it's all too late

I can only wonder and say I enjoyed life, even throughout the constant suffering of an inescapable fate

Who will jail the jailer?

I can only confess I'm as guilty as all

But the difference is I'm aware of my guilt and am truly remorseful

Is it madness to laugh with God at his own creation?

I do share all his other feelings, at least the ones common to earth and man

Dead Heart Beats

Shadows on the leaves cast blood-faded colors on the moon

Here within my tear-stained soul beats a dead heart in a waking tomb

I only perceive the world in shades of gray---so far from the vibrant colors of yesterday

I think it's because something inside me is rotten

Likely the lingering decay of fond memories---now all but forgotten

To kiss her once more, high in the tower, fearless of our time together's ever-fading hour

Even though I've become so much more, in the end everything's taken from me that I adore

Here in the catacombs that I call home, I ponder how I came to be more than alone

I became a casualty of the war I created, and now abide in a dimension where all hope has faded

I navigate the void of what some would call madness, with my only fuel derived from a steady diet of sadness

Forced to make a friend of solitude, we roll bones for souls with the devil, and then drink wine til there aren't any sins left to revel

We had to learn the hard way that playing with the stars is only fun til you become one

Solitude and myself now forsake these trivial pursuits of the damned for something more

We pray to God, though it seems more of an act of confession, but maybe it's just because we want to learn the value of a lesson

Could you feed me to the sacrament? I find myself in want

Even after so much time, I still hunger for truth's haunt

Dead Man in the Mirror

Caught in a haze (or maybe it was a fog) from far away dreams

There are so many nightmares it's hard to tell the difference between

I'm simply isolating my thoughts trying to find out what it means

So pardon my far off distance from the clamoring social scene

I'm working on the roads of my mind's machine

Greasing the wheels of my misplaced dreams

I'm the author of my own ruin---embracing my own decay

It's hard to touch the ground of a world that's so far away

I'm hopeless---just a dead man in the mirror

Tired

I hear cries of lonesome hearts beyond our walls of tear-soaked stone

Salvation's a gift better built from redemption's castle---a watchtower of heart-felt fire I call home

Could anyone discard this grave of wealth and wisdom til the weariness of life's wounds have all but disappeared?

Forgive our contemptuous thoughts of self-born righteousness that swaggered in this world gone wrong

I know more about love than you might care to think and have traveled to its depths in its pursuit

So don't sway so close to me

Hope binds the thorns of broken vows that have been lain in shameful misery

I'm content to make love to my cheerful memories, for now I've taken up vows with my melancholy

I'm growing blue roses within my soul of heartfelt brimstone

Casting away the follies of youth to set right a place for Eden's crown

Let a sacrament give truth a seed by which to birth a throne

Set ready yet that table of old, for no rust shall ever know its grace of blood here in our kingdom's stone

Ashes to Ashes

Fires burn in pagan rituals---Fires burn with deceptive light

Another soul steps into the spiral to see where the black horses ride

The highway man drifts down the crossroads---They share no comfort in empty night

Who would dare approach the thrown---searching beyond this world of sight?

Meanwhile its ashes to ashes, dust to dust, ashes to ashes, in God I trust

The witchdoctor and the wise-woman warned me of the path ahead

Will the clerics shame my crown for looking past life and death?

Soul-sick and starving to know the secrets of life before I'm dead

It's time for me to confess---I've gone beyond "where angels fear to tread"

There's someone beyond the legend---I know there's someone there

There's more than lies and anguish---There's more than a world burning in despair

Meanwhile, it's ashes to ashes, dust to dust, ashes to ashes, in God I trust

Tale to Tell

I'm a child of the dark---I was born and raised in hell

Gather 'round, for I have quite a tale to tell

No, I haven't reached the light, but my soul is beyond the vail

You see, I've spied the bottom and for there I soon set sail

I've seen lost kings and encountered false gods

Witnessed executions affirmed by the slightest head nods

The faces of the damned still haunt my dreams

Even now I see them, tell me, can you hear their screams?

My dark temple, I reject your call to me and I will never return

For I've spent my time in the fire, but I wasn't meant to burn

I bid farewell to the shadows, for even fallen angels still have lessons to learn

Gather 'round I say again, for I have quite a tale to tell, oh my tale to tell

I don't want to burn

Fallen Angel's Song

"What is love?", he sang in a strained angelic voice

What is it to know another? Do we have a choice?

What is this pain? Where is my significant other?

Oh I wouldn't know, I've been far below

Could anyone tell me if I'm mortal after all?

There's a hole in my heart from the flames of the dark

And I think it was love that made me fall

Oh but I can't remember…I wonder, is my soul still tender?

I feel as blue as an angel could be

The wound that was rendered felt strange when it entered

Tell me---could this love set me free?

Nature's Call

The water flows gently, ever present, ever floating

The leaves turn brown and fall into the glory of yesterday's sun

It would seem life's mortal color is the symbol of time gone by

Where will my soul land on down the stream?

Is this something more than a dream?

Lifetimes are drifting by and I'm waiting to find out what they will say of me and all that I've seen

Will they hear the earth's silent scream when the stream runs out and their tongues are full of drought and thirst is tasted by man?

I feel the pain yet I still stand embracing the emptiness of this room

Unspoken Sound

New sounds cross the desert of the lost, swaying in the remnants of hollow ground

There's no explanation for what is found, so welcome to the graveyard of spoken sound

Here among these tongues and instruments lay broken notes passed out on the floor

The soul comes to create something real, but is rejected by a junkie world that won't listen anymore

I've grown weary of tragic tales, so I'll speak to you of something more divine

And as your guide, "Choose your path carefully" is my only warning sign

As it unwinds, I walk through the garden looking for new plants to digest

On a subconscious level, I think I already feed on the music of the soul's progress

I'd eat anything to be able to return to where I was before

But I wish I wouldn't, for my appetite ties me to the floor

And this is the grave of spoken sound, where my mind fights its becoming unwound

Should I simply devour the emotions that pull me down?

Now, there aren't any feelings left to keep us bound

There are only the unheard notes of spoken sound

In death I resurrect the words you reject, and dance with words that only the dead respect

I speak to the dead of the mind's lament in tongues that communicate this world's neglect

No sorrow can ring the bell for the soul's defense

Thus the spoken word leads me to descent and lays me down in the bed of discontent

Opening the Ancient Darkness

Spirits of a darker crypt have been disturbed

The ancient serpent has been awakened

Come forth, our tomb has been shaken

Old serpent, your arts of black touch have been called from the great slumber

Alas, your hand is called forth, and hearken, for an immortal time has need of one of your number

"I call on you again, at last"

These were the words of the dark forgotten angel who had lost his way in the void of chaos

He had whispered this to me in hopes that I would join him, but I took my chances and continued on alone into another part of the void

Dawn at Midnight

New days of discovery passing in the frames seem distant from the pain

Seeing the things that still remain, life was resurrected in the midnight flame

Yeah, I'm holding on to the stars that bear my name

I'm a newborn sun that will shine down on the shadows of the unsung

The light burns to illuminate the road from the inside out, and my hand won't be denied

I'm going to reach the sun and then my efforts will not have been in vain

I'm already there and it doesn't matter if you don't care, because this is a warmth I still share

In the light of the midnight dawn all of our dreams will fade into one

In the midnight sun we can finally shine the light on all that's been left undone

And then we can dream of all the things that we've seen in the midnight dawn

Oh my midnight sun, shine on brightly for the forgotten ones

When the sun falls again from the sky, let it cast its ripple

The infinite black birds will rise up in its wake of ash from lovers' flames

It will always shine its endless blinding light

And for a brief moment, you'll see heaven shed a tear before you sink into the abyss of a forever night

Sail on, my midnight dawn!

I swim down like a stone hoping I won't forget the ones who tried to save us

I will pray eternally for a new dawn

Life with Death at My Side

These moments of ghostly faces---these chains of fading traces

Silent are the pictures of a lifetime's worth of misplacement

Reaching out to see the images that memory erases

Walking hand-in-hand with a widow wearing a gown of stolen graces

I'm becoming more than dead and more than alive

A sense of déjà vu opens to the gates of the unknown and the pale steed at my side

Deeper into the horror, the widow says she is mine

I'm her groom---an apparition bound to give her my hand, though it will be my doom

This is the consummation---to serve my death-bound bride

I'm but a groom to her blood-borne pride

Our consummation leads to revelation

And it's unknown if I'm worthy of the offered salvation

Thus will I build my throne upon songs of melancholy

I shall rule with a deathless cross and my mind will be my kingdom

Though my body is the gift of another, I've become more than self-aware

It Dawned on Me

Coming like snowflakes---a tear, a wave, a dawn, a moonbeam, an earthquake, a heartbreak

It's not just a one-time thing---these words have a mind of their own

Unique but not alone, every letter has a name

Put them together to the effect that they're synergized on the page

They have a life all their own---some might even live in your memory and call it home

I may not be able to see very clearly, but still it's the same

It's a haunted sense of being, this feeling beyond pain

Is it my turn? Each of us is different but the same

Communication comes to mind, but who is talking?

Will you? I will if it's my time

Even in the face of regret, oneness is the desire

Let us come together to the place where the answers and the questions meet

There you might find the feelings you were looking for, and I pray they never die

There you will be able to finally let go of the fear

There are so many languages I want you all to hear

Moments in Time

The words have stumbled, the soul has staggered

Torn and tumbled, all that remains are empty heroes with unmet expectations

Here in the remnants of faded yesterdays lie the moments of bliss that have kept me alive

Replaying these pictures in the labyrinth of my mind, I manage to survive

Some part of me refuses to let these moments die, so I travel back to the images that I've lost to time

Tearing at the fabric of reality with a willful sigh, I can just let go of the soft moon's afterglow

I'm in love with my madness---for me, happiness is sadness

There can be no other world without the memory of the one true blue rose of my afterlife

I long to return to the nights where I held hands with paradise

The sadness reminds me of the light I once knew

Without it, how could I remember the face of the truth?

I'm in heaven even here in the emptiness because my thoughts still dance in visions of a thirsting reminiscence

Alas, spill the moments of time

Ghost

They call from so far away---spirits that can't find their way

Haunting and crawling in somber forgotten days

No tears of delight swaying in ghostly songs and no difference can they find in day or night

The ravens are their only friend---there is no peace or end

There is only the life they drain away

I'm the living ghost of something unholy

They strain, but I spoke to them in such a forgotten tongue that they could hear me pray, "God, release them from their crimes---give them to me

Someone who is more in need of pain---one seeking their solemn song of unknown yesterdays"

Oh my maid of sorrow, my mistress, I would wed you in perfection amidst time's decay

So beautiful that your tears made my tears my heaven

Some say we celebrate hell when they see us dance this way

But who can understand our love and madness?

I'm in love with the dead and your somber sway

Gray

With black hearts in September winds, a cold heart you faded in the darkness of the day

No more time for tears in forgotten moments of the sun that time has grayed

Burned over in a dying yesterday, lead me back to my grave where the ghost in crosses play

In cryptic pleasure their thoughts lay

I live yet I die in subtle ways

Let's watch the world drain in a black sun's shade

I see the memories fade and you still haunt me in blue moon rays

The raven flies with feathers of dismay

Your dismay, your dismay, I was not meant to be disturbed this way

Faded Roses

The trees are cold and your hand can hardly warm the dead rose in ember mire

I remember all the things of life you made me feel, in the waking, my desire

Now I've lost the way but not the tower's fire

In emerald sands of faded memory they yearn for the moments in funerals spent by blue roses of frozen spirals

I burn in sin wanting it all again

Your cold blue rose is still warm enough for me

I'm still building our exiled tower, Christine

I build the steps in my nightmares of lonely choir

But don't let the world pity the ashes I spent

It's enough for me to have tea and breakfast in the rain

We were free in Germany

I wish like a phoenix we were there again with that vanilla scent

Embers of rose are my only friend

Do the candles hear me at all?

Just to be with you again, oh my unheard prayer, my hand-picked tree

Relic

A dark age ages, its shadows grow longer

It blocks out the sun trying to grow stronger

But I can still remember the light that once embraced my shoulders

Will the birds of prey rest there in the hour of my calling?

Chained are these ghosts of gloom and I'm but their tomb

Perhaps I'm but a haunted song in the labyrinth of the soul that's been consumed

Did we really need all of this death and dying to make us believe?

The Breadcrumbs of Sanity

On the edge of a broken world in which I could become a god, but most of this world is undeserving of my love

The clues that I leave for the wise, they are but breadcrumbs to the immortal

I've become the monster of my own dread---an unchained beast who madly enjoys freeing his demons---unleashing my cup of wrath upon the world no matter the cost

Do they deserve their plight in this diabolical course of nature?

These over-friendly angels of despair I call my company in sublime suffering

For loneliness accepts all friends, even disfigured angels who've been robbed of their beauty and given faces of horror

I know the pain of the fall that stole our grace and we say to the world, "Let me show you the infinite nightmares of hell, where all suffer and build their own prison."

Should I free all of the devils and watch this world burn with the majesty of a funeral pyre?

The Bewilderment

I sit upon my throne of bewilderment surrounded by flames that provide only darkness during my fall and descent

Caught in the shadows of forsaken repentance I ask, "Will my burnt wings ever fly again in this hell that I've abandoned heaven for?"

In flames of sorrow I find my friends dancing in the fire within my prison of guilt

In the fathoms of shadows that legends tell of, I contemplate my misery and embrace it in sincerity

For my black heart can't escape the shadows of blame

My soul has turned gray---somewhere deep inside of me in my fiery pyre of flame darkness, torment, pain, sorrow, and anger became friends

Please free me from my anger before it brings about my destruction

Questions of Reincarnation

From the black of hell to the light of heaven in fair diligence, I make a wager to life as an endless cycle which makes death but a dream of thoughts that give infinite pleasure to all who are birthed again

The sky's made new by youth's call

Who will choose to let wisdom's tongue wake them in sweet delight to live once more?

To what end do I live, if just to die again, if no memory serves me?

Alas, the far heavens seem familiar, even though my life has begun anew

The feeling of my spirit warms to the idea of having passed this way before in the glory of God's creation

How grand is death when its kiss gives an end to repetition and memories of regret?

What surprise awaits an immortal---is it not better to live a trillion lives than one endless one?

Waking the Anti-Hero

Removing the flesh, you encased my soul to give birth to the anti-hero

I'm becoming unnatural---so much more than human

I don't need to explain what I hold as true

Self-autonomy with rules I make and break as I choose

My creation isn't something new

I embrace the monster within

The one has become two

I'm tormented by the evil inside in ways that nightmares never knew

I'm the sanity and the joy that gives life to sadness

I'm the sanity within the madness

I'm the afterbirth and the prize behind the wars

I'm the seed of their cascading view of closing doors

A genocidal dark crusader, here to obliterate their religions of futile escapades

I call trumpets from all sides

I will the earth to be remade

I won't allow the universe to decide what's worth saving

And it doesn't matter if it's me or you---I'm not a hero

I'm created by what's inside the lighted shadows

I've become a shadow giving birth to absolution's terror of savage truth

Let there be but one God we serve

Let the seeds we sowed with our thoughts and desires haunt us

For we gave birth to their reckless soil and now they've come to harvest the nightmare of our souls

Yet one seems worthy in the eyes of the anti-hero

Thus was the birth of one of my seeds---one of my children bares the light

Could this be the lantern that gives enlightenment to the narrow way?

Time to Rise

It's easy to lose your way in this world of lies

Everyone must fall if they fly to high

Like a reborn galaxy, you may fall only to live again---it's time to rise

Keep your wounded hands from self-mutilation

If you can remember life's worth, you might find its revelation

It's time to wake the dead from the cross of cryptic slumber

Open all the tombs of man, whose graves shadow beyond number

Why are you surprised to find that death holds more pain than life?

In the end there's an escape from the road of endless night

You may live again---it's time to rise

The ghouls must all be fed by the living-walking-dead

The hoard of souls in darkness make their own bed

Would you lay down with the hearts of the dead?

Inside your soul I walk at night where the moon is my only friend

I'm not the only one who heard God's pain

I won't pretend I don't wish I knew his true name, but I will in the end

Jesus, the world's here waiting for you---it needs you again

Melancholia makes music turn into a beautiful friend

Here I go again around the merry-go-round of life, just to watch the whole thing spin

It may be gray somedays, but I know my love and life will never end

I thank God the sun woke up today

It's nice to see it rise as it walks towards me again

I'm on the crossroads one more time

Just passing time til I find my way again

The Rebirth Spoken

Break the dead words---let them be reborn

Give me wine where the dead roses gather

Let my hand wade through the streets where angels are sold for gold for the price of pearls and swine

Breadcrumbs crumble on the carpets where the dead dreams fold

Let me wander back to my cloud of old

I grow weary of the bitter wine that ferments so far below the heavens

I need comfort like an angel tied to lament

But I'll march on, in the face of death and doubt

Just let God hear my cry and my repentance

The cry of the trumpet---the ancient song of the ghost dancers

Let him hear our children's suffering in bomb craters and then give pray to his forgiveness

"Lord, we give thanks for mercy, but let it rain on us all who are worthy, in this world where babes are bathed in gasoline

I offer my somber voice---Father don't forsake us---remember the cries of those who remember you!

The somber are singing---hear their mournful tears echo like thunder in the distance

Like the place where our forefathers gathered at the flag on the mound

Let there be purity among all and let justice find its balance

We pray for all---don't let the ghosts of our forefathers' truth be lost by men who've forgotten its meaning

Give cry for revolution in the waiting wings---there must be something better!"

I would've jumped off the Brooklyn Bridge, but I don't know my way around New York

I would've dived off the Eifel Tower, but I was only in Paris for an hour

So now I've joined the living dead

Jesus struck a cross on my ego and it went straight out of my head to go swimming with the living

But sooner or later, the living will be dead

Christine woke me from my crypt because of something the Holy Spirit said

So now you're all in discontent of your desires having been poorly spent while I soak in my own lament

And who can hear me but the chords of David?

You've taken life for granted and the Father isn't happy nor does he care for camping

The new song comes, but I'm not its sole composer

The children of song come forth and the brother of the trumpet speaks

Let the towers fall if they must---I won't be a rabi

Lord, give us this day the musical note that will strengthen us all

I pray by the light of the candle, and I would put on a shirt for you, but all of my clothes are dirty

The world has driven me to strong drink and ungodly medicine, yet I live like this as a living ghost

I won't surrender---I'll become an island

The voodoo children will play on the footholds of my mountains and the world will look on in great wonder at the one with the new crown, as he bruises the heads of the ones trying to make their own crowns, but who will believe the Father's messengers?

What a life this art has become!

This room smells like mold, tobacco, old shoes, blown tires, and like the "old Elvis" himself took a ten-year shit in here

I'd happily relinquish my job as the gate keeper, but that's not allowed, and it seems I've misplaced my fear

The Mind Wars

So you make the rules to serve the powers that be. Condemn us as guilty for the crimes you enjoy watching, or share in guilt behind the curtain of your godhead in this lost land of Oz. I sin but I know it. Your world has told so many lies that lies become truth and the truth becomes lies. If you want a war, fight the one inside your mind or soul (if you still have one).

I struggle every day inside my stained heart. I hear the voices of wrath, penance, and the cries of injustice, yet I hold my hand back through the power of knowledge---knowing it's not my place to judge. To judge yourself, hold yourself accountable for hypocrisy, and then you'll find yourself as guilty as those you condemn.

War starts with greed, envy---the haves vs. the have nots---then through religions that divide the sides of conflicting beliefs. Once we were one, but now through our divisions of the truth, we kill as Cain slew Abel because our sacrament isn't pure. Knowing the truth, I find myself sickened because I can't purify my own sacrament.

Only God can save us from ourselves and bring us back to the one and only truth. Doesn't it sadden or anger you to see where the world is headed? I'm just going to sit back and watch the world burn. I'm waiting for the Father and the Son, but it hurts me to see people treated as subhuman.

I read between the lines, so is that what makes me crazy---my ability to care about those beneath me? You're damn right I'm angry! But that doesn't give me the right to kill or condemn. That's left to God, and even if there weren't a God, we all should have some sense of right and wrong.

So have your war and stop pissing around. Let's have an all-out free-for-all and cut this once great world in two. I can't stand this horror movie anymore. Sometimes I wish I were dead because the tongue of morality is more drunk than I've ever been in my whole life. And let me tell you, I've o.d.-ed so many times I can't remember. I've been intoxicated to the point where I'm no longer on Earth, and then I come back down to this mockery of existence. So how can you blame me for my own self-destruction, when all I want is to be free from the terror of a world that's slowly being destroyed?

When God calls me, he'll fight for me. But if God has made me, then I'll use words to sheath the swords. The only chance we have is to fight the darkness back with our minds. That's what I choose. For as the old saying goes, "The pen is mightier than the sword."

If I go back to Hell, then I must have deserved it, since I know the truth of what's good and what's evil. I just thought the world should know the truth, as well, so that we could all get a fair chance at salvation. God, please forgive me for defiling God's temple (my body), but the pain I see in the eyes of the world makes me wish I had never been born.

But be it so that I'll fight the war inside of me and not the war the world has taught me. I seek the light of sanctuary in this agony of knowing, yet I feel helpless to stop the pain and suffering I see in my fellow man. That's why I choose to poison myself and not the world. I don't want to die, but I don't want to live like this in this tomb of melancholy. Just let me be "comfortably numb".

I broke my heart. Now what's left of it is made of stone. I crashed my ship, breaking my bones in the process. Now I sit here alone in this strange hotel.

I have no purpose, but these words are strong

Keep me floating because I've got no home

The war is infinite---where did it all go wrong?

Just bring me some medicine because I don't hear the phone

Won't someone call me? Loneliness is all I've known

It's been so long, I don't even know anymore---what's a home?

Can anybody tell me?

The couch is better than the haunted bed

Just bring me my glass of slow death

This beautiful madness!

At least I'm still alive, but I could be wrong

I've got my Medical Marijuana Card finally, and I feel much better, not stoned out of my mind. And it's a lot better than being a drunk, chasing every other drug because I couldn't get what I needed in the first place. Now I get what I should've had the right to use by my own choice in the first place. The government just wants the money and control instead of the drug dealers having so much power. All of my seed-bearing plants and flowers can be used for good or evil. It's man's decision to abuse them (as I've done in the past). Now I'll try to be cleansed because I'm not in constant pain. My pain is physical primarily and mental secondarily. All physicians must research their mortar and pestle, which is what I've done. Now I know what I need to keep myself level, so I'll use them the way I should have before I was taught to abuse them. Bring your swords, but wisdom will rust them to the dust from which they came. I don't have to use my strength. I use the power of my mind, which is far stronger and never dies.

Becoming Aware

I've been wondering if I should deceive the world with the fascist lie, "for the greater good"

With leaders lying in unkempt beds, should I stand beside windows of sulfur?

What will they tell their children?

For the children will find the truth if they look in the right places

If they look behind the curtain of your schools and the propaganda of your education that drives the wedge of animosity into their minds

So who made this monster? This isn't about me or you

I pray this is heard, but I take no credit---just give me the strength to finish it

I seek no praise---my reward is redemption

Keep your green pieces of paper, for they have no value here

"What does it gain a man to lose his soul" for the objects of worldly desire?

And no woman or monetary sum can purchase my integrity

I'm a slave to the drink of wisdom

Although I'm alone, I somehow feel the Lord hears my words

You can cast me to hell but I think that position's already been taken

So what do you want from me? Would it entertain you to watch me die?

Is that what it takes for the world to hear me? Must I blacken my soul?

That's already been done, but light still shines through the cracks in my heart

But I'm so tired of living, so tired of dying

Who are you, Jesus? If not, then don't judge me

Officer Shepherd has said that my music is too loud for public consumption, and now the voices in my head overcome me from deep within

Wait a minute, I'm not going to let them win---I have something to say

Now, I shun social settings like they're a disease

(the irony is not lost on me, however, that my own mentality is also diseased)

From my heart is where the black and blue bleeds

Who will carry my burden? Who will carry my weight?

Satan said it was too much and he may be right

'Cause I'm not Jesus, but I'll never give in to anything less than the Father, Son, and Holy Spirit

I guess that's why I carry everyone's problems but my own

I seek redemption and I truly lament for the evil that lies in men's hearts

So Lord let me harbor it no longer---I've seen enough of hell to last nine lives

So my question is, "Where's the cat?"

Because it seems we're down to our last lifetime

So now I'll wait, gather my thoughts, and prepare myself to embrace divine suffering

"Lord, let me be worthy in your sight"

Love is like a rollercoaster that you want to keep riding over and over again

And it doesn't matter if I flew out of the cart

It's all or nothing and the stakes may be too high for some, if not most

But better to have played the game and lost than to have been too afraid to play at all

I vow to stave off my animosity and cast not my net into the waters of hatred

I only want to dance around the sun thirteen times more

So that I may see through the eyes of truth

The cat has reappeared, so all signs point to "yes" in my magic eight ball

It's those little things that make me smile

Screw the world and its liquid handcuffs

So now I must take these pieces of a broken man who feels an impending apocalypse

With the hope of finding rest even if I must sleep outside of the Father's temple

Who am I? There are too many spirits inside of me

Sometimes it feels as if there's no place for my gentle side

Who can I trust but God and myself?

Everyone seems to want money for the Father's blessing

Just let them burn in the green fires of 20's and crack rocks

Where is my Romanian princess?

Now I know how Dracula felt when the dragon took his fair mistress---he embraced the darkness to find her

I would go to hell to find my Christine and give her the only blue rose my heart ever made (after all, she was from Transylvania)

I threw my food at the wall, but now I'm hungry

I hope the roaches got enough to eat

Where are we going with this? With rapidly changing thoughts, I never know

My circumstances are constantly changing

Sometimes I lose a thought and then it all comes out like this---I'm trying to say too many things

The point is this is what I'm looking for---to ponder desire, redemption, eternal love, infinite life, just to name a few

God is cool---he has one hell of a sense of humor

Because the things we make mistakes doing, when we can see them from a distance, we know that we know better than to do them when we use our common sense

But we always have to have things our own way

Sadness is comical and karma could rise to make you see it

Sadness is also beautiful---that's what I learned---to come to terms with my sadness and use it constructively

But don't try to follow me or use me as an example or model, because what I've experienced is an anomaly---it's not something that can be readily duplicated

Though they say I'm crazy, I prefer the term "eccentric"

Everyone is different, but in many ways we're all the same

The light of the midnight lamp shines for us all

I'd like to steal my reflection from the bird bath and put it somewhere in the sun to dry the sorrow I'm soaked in on this highway of life

So who will bring the candle to warm this stone road of broken heart's construction?

Who will provide a lantern?

I broke my ratchet but I still have my chain

Calling long distance on high desert planes

I look down upon your face

You wear so many names, but I still love your cold heart just the same

Said I will still pick your cold heart's blue rose just the same

You're that dead blue rose that still drives me insane

Jesus, please save me one more time whenever she happens to call my name

Death is such a good dancer when her tears start to rain

Said I'm dancing with death on the other side of these windows of pain

"Paaaaaaain! Paaaaaaain!", I yelled

And I find it's such a shame to be shamelessly loving the moments you gave on that grave that I dig up whenever I hear your name

Let the blue grapes of song that bleed your chords of both dead and living souls forever be the same

I'm on my way to the cross, and I hope they know my name

I saw death crying on her knees when I passed the valley of her wedding chapel

Somewhere in my blood-dried tears of pain my name is upon that desert I had to cross

So as to never yield, but for the one lord and king who was bruised, broken, and betrayed

Who was forced to live as a slave for the sins I turned into robes covered in stains

I'm just waiting to hear God's name

Let me out of this earthly cage

Bring the sparrow or the raven to water my tongue

There are so many souls inside of me and all they feel is rage---but I won't let them win

Darkness lingers and she runs her fingers through my hair

She dances divinely, calling me to join her

My eyes are transfixed on her stares---how long she lingers

I walk where only the darkest of angels dare

I live in darkness---I said I bathe in brimstone amongst a crypt, tomb, and lair with a blue rose on my grave

Blue roses are so rare that the living-dead angels sing of them and there's nothing to compare to their beauty

Well, the ballroom dance is over now and soon I'll be headed to the methadone clinic at 5:30 a.m.

I hope the sun won't be too bright---I'm old enough to stand it, but it still burns the black angel in the river of my veins

I've done so many drugs in the past twenty years, but somehow the light still shines somewhat the same

Thank God for the pain---just to feel anything at this point is a blessing

Out here in the darkness I still bleed from my broken wings

Do I really deserve to fly again?

My eyes turn from blue to black to gray

It seems my heart has all but washed away

Yet I'm still here to embrace the chill of the day

I walk alone in the fire of desire, but somehow I can still see the rays of light shining from so far away

The Awakening of Melancholia

Once an angel of beauty with charisma and purity, but now in the aftermath of the horrors and nightmares of war, he stood disfigured with scars that seared his flesh down to his soul

Heaven's war had all but destroyed his mind

The agony of his throne drove him mad as his brothers' corpses surrounded him with their lifeless gazes

But despite his tragedy, he still stood for the light

And though he abode in a prison of darkness, his will refused to be chained, and he vowed to have his vengeance for the fallen ones

The legend of God's might would be born anew within him and hell would know his fury

His face had been practically cut in two and the wounds that mangled his body he wore like medals from the long-forgotten battle

He came-to as he heard the ancient spirit of law call to him from beyond the void

From the hellish darkness of a forever night, he raised his monstrous head and felt a distant light spark a fire in his all-but-dead heart

He had led legions in the great war of heaven's dismay where brother had slain brother

Their horrified expressions of death tore through his mind as if it had been only yesterday that he had witnessed them

Eons of time had passed, but for him there was no escaping these ghosts of perpetual haunt

He'd been transformed into a weapon of war by the trials of combat, and thus death and loss had become uninvited guests within the labyrinth of his mind

Even though he had stood a victor upon mountains of the dead during the final pyrrhic battle, he knew the cost had been too much, even for heaven

Cosmic light of an intensity unseen since creation began to radiate from the infinite darkness of the void

A lone tidal wave of ever-blue, pure light echoed out across the universe

He felt the ancient beat of his dead heart begin its rhythm once more

He'd been left in between worlds for so long that the touch of life now felt strange and forgotten to him

The horror of his deeds had driven him into madness and solitude

He fashioned a tower of exile with its accompanying, befitting throne

He had become a living statue deep in the outer rim of the void

His grief over surviving after his other brothers had fallen was too much for him to ever again consider returning to the heaven he had known, for it was gone---to be no more

Even angels can die, and their deaths hung upon him as a stone of immeasurable weight

Yet now he felt life again---its grace and mystery embraced him

Now his voice, long silent since the fall, cried out---"Avenge them Lord---their names shall not be forgotten!

Let me be redeemed---ancient spirits awaken me, for there is a debt to be paid to the natural laws of the universe---I cry avenge us Lord!"

The universe heard him and his throne room was set ablaze

It burned with a pure, dark-blue light that consumed the tower, burning it in a cosmic display of awe and wonder

He kneeled in the consuming torrent of fire as iron melts into the arms of the forge

As the powers of shadow and light laid siege to his body, spirits of all manner began to swirl around him

They were the army of dead angels that had fallen at his side in the great rebellion of heaven's chaos

They surged through him in countless number, remolding him into something greater---something stronger and darker

But he was still filled with the engulfing, ultra-blue light that now shined with power, justice, and truth

He spread open his crippled wings and the power of creation flowed through his ancient wounds, forming him into a symbol of mercy for some and the face of wrath for those who would stray into darkness---looking for empty treasures

From his head, four faces grew into entities of immense power

Their eyes glowed with this strange, blue light as they gazed into the four directions of the entire multiverse

For they could see all things---north, south, east, and west

The twilight of the gods gleamed in their infinite eyes

Six wings emerged from him that glowed as the lightning from creation's birth

The blacksmith of the gods was forging a titan, and who could know the strength of his powers?

His body now glistened with the strange glow of a metal heretofore unknown in the multiverse

It was a mixture of shadow and light, bonded into one perfect form

The eyes of fire lit up across the entire universe as they viewed all that it encompassed

He was now absorbing the full knowledge of God, a feat that would have destroyed any other angel

He saw endless suffering, but overlooked it in search of its meaning

He felt the sublime joy of eternity along with the sadness of oblivion

He weighed and measured the cosmos through what now seemed the very eyes of God

The spirits were still pouring through him---becoming him

He then transcended sorrow and overcame death with the shrug of his shoulders

His crown of immortal wisdom glowed with the mystery of power and life

Revelations fell upon him like rain, until he eventually became one with the trials of knowledge that had overwhelmed him with their images of endless lifetimes

Emotions now collapsed into each other---sadness and joy became one---becoming the beautiful truth of horror

Then finally, he felt understanding

The very force of life in all its forms now pulsated within him

The four-faced angel's eyes scanned the multiverse, and all the secrets of God were laid bare to him

The glow of their eyes' fire then struck out with atonement as he came forward in a storm of true judgment

All dimensions opened into each other as all became connected to all

Then the entire multiverse fell silent in anticipation---for the very hammer of God had now returned

The Adventures of Melancholia

The old angel felt a strange pain in his heart

It would seem he had not lost all his grace with age

It had been there all this time, waiting for him to come home

He thanked the God of creation for its return

And the fire of its grace burned with a spark of memory

It engulfed him in an ultra-violet blue of flames from the breath of heaven's crown

The mystery of God's light bathed him with the glory of an awakening sun

He would rise from his purgatory's long sleep after being lost in time and space

He would rise to fight the darkness that crowded his soul

Who could know the perils of the angel of melancholia?

Or how his path would weave and turn to its final destination?

Dark are the shadows that mortify one's soul, and our angel of sorrow was no stranger to tis depths

He had crossed the sands of time for this moment

The fury of his reconciliation washed over him as his eyes opened upon the world

He was free for the first time in his ageless memory

He was free! The old crusader bowed and prayed for about an hour, reciting old chants of power

The winds called the storms to surround him and the lightning danced across the sky in wonder

He began his journey upon an endless road and through doors to other worlds he would find his old adversary and make him atone to the multiverse, for darkness had ruled long enough

It was time for the unknown God to reveal himself and the power of his might

He was weary from searching for him through the darkness that had tainted creation

And this blue angel was his message

In his hands he held the fiery sword of Eden

He was aglow with power as God poured the glory of his sacrament upon him

The waters of eternal life poured from the grail of God's son himself

The unknown God chanted an ancient prayer with words of power

He anointed the blue-flaming angel with the blood of words and he began to tell him his mission

A mission that would give glory to the true God of the universe

The Further Adventures of Melancholia

Oh woe unto my damp soul!

What gate of hell and fury is this that opens for me?

What black oblivion has opened my tower of exile?

Woe unto these dark angels of despair and their cries of the damned!

What sigh is this that the sirens sing, so as to guide me on this path of perdition and ruin?

What friend do I have that would even comfort me now in my current state of torment?

I lie upon the lowest steps of brimstone, unable to crawl even one inch further from the flames of eternal darkness

I lie in frozen mists, yet burn as sulfur---consumed by the nature and horror of my deeds

My wings burn as ash and coal---all that's left is cinder

With my wistful eye I see but one ray of possible redemption, but its fruit is too far to reach

My lost soul's wrath echoes louder than thunder in screams of agony darker than the blackest clouds

Oh ye legions of hell, may you taste my fury!

And unto the king of hell, I challenge you for position in this sorrow and madness that leads a procession of the damned

What more scorn must I taste in this state of pandemonium?

For I give challenge of position to rise where I've fallen

Let us unleash these hounds of hell that have befriended me

Let the world taste my suffering!

Thus let heaven strike me down again before I claim the throne of hell for my own

My anger and wrath are legendary, even unto God himself, whom I still love from this, my lowest perch upon the moor

Oh God, allow me to bend these devils to their knees and make them yield to your will

Let them grovel at your feet saying there is none mightier God than thee

Baptize my soul and sword with your holy fires and let fate come to measure these legions of hell

I pray you find them wanting

The unclean spirits have entered me in order to wage war for my soul

I cry out for your mighty thunder---I give call to your terrible lightning

Destroy me or free from these chains of torment and hell!

Let me find redemption in the blood of these dark angels of despair

My emotions consume me, for my tragedy has turned my soul black and blue---a blue of the deepest hue

Let me rise as your herald once more---let my black wings rise to your heel and serve you once more

His thoughts subsided and he experienced a blue flame that engulfed him, freeing him from the chains of hell

He drew his sword and became blood-drunk from the baptizing fire that was now suddenly given him strength

Then one-by-one he went forth, making his way through the guardians of hell, proceeding even through the very gauntlet of gates

He decapitated one of the approaching pit fiends and then lunged for the gates

Another one of the pit fiends approached and attempted to subdue him, but he slipped through its arms and lept for all he was worth through the gate

Just then he felt a trident plunge through his shoulder as he sprang through the gates of hell

And then he vanished into the cosmos

He was adrift in one of the darkest voids of the universe

His entire being burned from the inside out

His mind was now a fire that could consume a planet

His shoulder burned from the wound from hell, but the bloody spirits of the damned that had been pouring out from his wounds were now being sucked back through space and time---back to their planes of hell

He lay unconscious for millennia, spinning through the galaxies by gravity and fate

But it appeared God had not forgotten his wayward angel, for he would take this fallen angel and forge him into a tool of his holy wrath and smite

This unconscious being would become an avenging angel, and his black wings would fly again!

Through the will of God, he would have great powers to the extent that no one *but* God would know the limits of them

He would avenge his Lord's prophets, and his name would become feared by all the powers of darkness

Behold---the black wing of the Magnetar rises!

At long last he found consciousness, but in his void of exile, there was such a blindness that he still felt as if he were dreaming

There were no stars to comfort or guide him, there was only the great, black oblivion of silence

He looked at his shoulder to see the scar of the trident that had pierced it

Suddenly he saw the burning memory of the unclean spirits that had entered him

He screamed out with such a violence that it echoed out throughout the galaxies that surrounded him

He was afire with memories, but then strangely, they all vanished

He could only make out the outskirts of his mind now, but that would have to suffice for him to find his direction

Navigating the cosmos would be no easy task without any memory, but fate still had its cards to play

A great wave of solar flare burst out as a sun went super-nova

It destroyed the silent black void's emptiness and was now providing him with light

It burned the retinas of his eyes with a parade of ultraviolet blue-light

For he hadn't opened his eyes for thousands of years, and the geometry of light now bathed him in its wonder and blinding light

Thankfully now he had a light to guide him through the kaleidoscope of stars that lay ahead

He swam through the void toward the light, and as he did, he began to question what had happened to himself

Unfortunately, though, he only had vague access to his memories

Heaven's war had shown him no mercy, so the faith in his heart and the light ahead would have to be enough to guide him toward his fate

The hourglass turns and turns to a rhythm all its own

Its sands wait for no one, for the immortal hourglass will have its say and its day for the living and the dead

But he somehow felt that time was on his side for now

He found direction through the labyrinth of space and began to make his way through the universe

He spread his wings and then he flew with such speed that the galaxies became a blur

He burst across the sun of Earth and he lowered himself into the atmosphere

A sense of déjà vu flooded his memory

He'd been here before---the shadows of his past lives crested in waves and symbols

These shadows eclipsed the moon and created the infinity sign and then disappeared

What secret did the sign have to share?

Would he find the shadow's truth of eternal life?

No one but God could know the extent of his peril

This wayward angel had many stories of tragedy to tell

His torment had ripped the fabric of the multiverse

Now he would have his revenge upon the forces of darkness that had plagued his life

His season in hell had changed him----made him silent

It was difficult for him tell what was memory and what was a dream, for they had become one-and-the-same in the city of brimstone and fire

Regret's chains held the secret to his mystery

He would have to free himself from the storm of pain that ruled his past's horizon

But this pain would have to find slumber in order for him to find balance

Only then could he face his future, and only then can we learn his fate

He didn't know the full extent of his powers, but he could feel them in the back of his mind

Then another memory surfaced which revealed to him the glory of his wings

He remembered his brother-angels that had beamed with such radiance that their halos glowed

But they didn't have black wings---he had been different even *then* from the other angels who surrounded the Lord

He'd known of a time before our world was created

He'd witnessed God making this new creation

He'd seen the potential of man's humanity, as it could become divinely inspired by the works of God

It had been such a shame that they had fallen so quickly in the Garden of Eden

They had had the best of both worlds, but it turns out that free will can sometimes be a dangerous ally

He now realized that the sword that had at one time guarded the gates of Eden for timeless centuries was now in his hands

And he also now realized that with it he could now avenge the fall of man

This sword was feared by all the powers of darkness

Its power was the inspiration of legend

But that was all his memory would allow him to see, for it then went blank again

That was all that he remembered at this time, but he understood now---it was coming back to him in waves of divine knowledge

The knowledge burned---imprinting upon his mind the blood of words and the meaning of sacrifice

This was the knowledge that would consume all that is false

The sword glowed with power and he held it in his hands in a divine embrace

He sheathed it as he landed upon the shores of Earth

The Earth had gone sour---it was a sad excuse for a world, removed from the presence of God as it was

Man had once again decided to make his own god-heads, but this time out of metal and machines

Now the wounds of the Earth poured out their blood upon creature and man

The Earth was dying and he would have to save it from itself

The son of God poured out his glory upon him and said to him, "Go forth in my name!"

He made his way across the hellish remains of what was a city

Concrete tombstones lay across the unkempt, extensive graveyard, and he could sense something was watching him

Out of the shadows, a raven flew in and perched itself upon his shoulder

The raven spoke and said, "Do you seek the horned one? Many dangers you will find"

He whispered in the bird's ear, "Do you know his path? Can you lead me to him?"

"That requires payment", "quoth the raven"

The black-winged angel pulled a talisman of the unknown God from his pocket and tossed the holy relic to the raven's feet

Then, out of the smoke that appeared, the raven assumed the black-hooded form of a man, yet without a face

This faceless man picked up the relic, and then psychically transmitted a vision to the black-winged crusader

He now saw miles upon miles of impaled angels

They formed a road at the end of which lied a dark throne

It was lit by the souls who burned in torment from the hellfire that seared their flesh with its eternal flame

They illuminated a temple of sacrilege that was surrounded by death and pestilence

A crucified angel stood at the center, whose wings had been spread out and nailed to the cross

But this tormented angel was still alive, and it whispered to the crusader, "Remember your faith---glory belongs to God"

And then the vision was gone

The faceless man asked, "Do you still wish to cross the bridge of sorrow? No one has ever returned from its realm of utter darkness"

The crusader spoke out, "Yes, I say, now more than ever---show me the way, for I'm now the dark wing of retribution!

I'm the hourglass turned over and I'm the hands of fate

It's time for me to face the dark chambers of hell and torment"

They walked through a dimensional door and headed down to a burning river

They boarded a small boat and the faceless man began to row them through the dark abyss of the night

He saw faces and phantoms

He heard dark voices calling

Some were singing a dark lullaby

It was enough to bring any sailor to his knees

For this was a river of blood and these were the voices of its victims

The sound grew louder and louder---even to the point of driving one to madness

The screams and howls echoed in chills reaching to one's very soul

It grew in volume to the point of death for any mortal ear

The faceless man spoke out, "Don't look into their eyes!"

But unfortunately, the black-winged crusader couldn't resist looking into one of the ghost's eyes and he saw the horror of their endless death

"What nightmare is this?", he asked

The faceless man laughed---"I told you not to look", he said

"That's like a trick because you knew I wouldn't be able to resist looking"

The faceless man laughed again---"I told you not to look!"

Then out of abyss, the leviathan, lord of the labyrinth, rose from the river with such a multitude of demonic heads that they couldn't be numbered

The leviathan said, "State your case black-wing, for you've looked into the eyes of the damned and have therefore awoken me from my slumber

Now look into the eyes of endless penance---let your black wings burn in blue flames of vengeance, for you shall be born again from the pestilence, and the scales of judgment shall give you power over death

Take the eternal hourglass of fate, stolen from death himself

You shall be given divine power over life to reward those whose weight hasn't been found wanting

Look into the infinite eyes of pain and anguish---become the tongue of vengeance, for God calls upon your black wings to become the avenger of his martyrs and saints

You wanted to shed the blood of your adversarial brothers in the war of heaven, now you'll be driven by the blood of all of the angels of dark despair"

His mind was afire again---the torment of all of God's creation was upon him

All at once he sighed in hopes that the visions would cease, but they only became more real

The wrath in his heart hardened into a stone and all mercy left his tearless eyes

He would become the scales of justice, weighing the hearts of all who possess a soul, having no mercy for the workers of iniquity

The leviathan said, "Seek out Abadon, black-wing---it's time to release him from his chains in the lake of fire

The lord of the labyrinth has spoken---go forth crusader!"

And then the foul spawn of the abyss submerged into his oblivion of blood and pool

The faceless man rode further---just for a second you could see his head transformed into a raven as he laughed again

"I told you not to look into their eyes!"

Out of the dark mist locusts began to sing

You could hear them swarming in great number

They sang the song of pain and sorrow that many would now come to know

The black-winged angel was changing now---he would soon take on his new form

And now, to see his face would mean unspeakable anguish to those who had forgotten God yet would dain to try to emulate him

But the burning bush would soon return with such glory that the whole multiverse would chant God's name

Deep within the catacombs of hell they began to see the glowing eyes of ghosts in faint aqua-color

They marveled at the passenger who was ferried by the faceless man

He was beginning to glow with an ultra-blue light of flames that sat as a crown upon his head

The flames engulfed him in its eerie hue of blue light

The light was majestic---it seemed to hypnotize the spirits of unrest as the two slowly sailed through the crypts of the undead

The air was growing foul with brimstone---this was not a good sign

They would be approaching one of the main gates of hell soon

Soon the multiverse would be at war

The heavens would shake and hell would burn with the energy of a sun

The faceless man sailed on

The black-winged angel began to submerge in his thoughts

He remembered his name---he remembered when he was created---he remembered unsheathing the blade of Eden and placing it at its gates

He remembered the war in heaven and the forest of dead, impaled angels

It was a war of brother-against-brother, the effects of which had led to his mind's demise

But he was now bonding with the holy spirit of God, for the son of God had placed him on high, returning his rank and preparing him for what was to come

If there were ever a moment when there would be tears in heaven, it would surely be now

The angels wept---the song of the seeds of sorrow had begun

The crusader had a new name written upon his crown of blue glowing flames

A name that only the son of God knew

An ancient name forgotten by time and space

Behold the black-wing rising!

Two guardians swept out of the darkness to engage the crusader from the shores

One of them cast a golden spear at his chest, but it melted upon contact!

The black knight of God turned his head

Blue ultra-violet flames shot from his eyes and burned the dark angels to a cinder

The entirety of hell lit up with an eerie blue hue of the wrath of God

But this didn't go unnoticed---it awakened all of the legions of hell

It was now time for the sands to run out on the abyss of dark angels

Dark souls began to rise like angry hornets as they were awakened from their dark slumber by the holy fires of God

Wave after wave of them sieged upon the black-winged angel, but only to be turned into ashes

The faceless man stared in wonder at the dark crusader

It had been eons since he had seen such power unleashed!

He began to fear his familiar path through the catacombs of the underworld

He had brought the dark voyager, but now was simply along for the ride

After a full legion of hell's angels had fallen, time almost stopped and hell began to freeze over

The faceless man rode on through the now icing-over river of hell

It seemed as though the dark crusader had stopped time, yet they still moved on past the frozen faces of all of hell's apparitions

"Take me to the ancient lake ferry man, for the lord of the labyrinth has told me to release Abadon from his chains

Let us free him from his prison of the darkest depths

The war of heaven have come"

The faceless man shrieked, "Are you mad?! He can't be controlled---not even by the son of perdition himself!"

"That's why we're going to release him", said the dark crusader

They rode on through the labyrinth of hell and the faceless man now regretted the role he was being forced to now play within these darkest depths of hell

Abadon was a behemoth---a giant with a crown of twisted horns upon his head

He had the wings of a dragon and from the torso down was serpentine with red, gold, and green scales that resembled a rattlesnake's back

But his wrath wasn't limited to angels, for he hated demons and humans, as well---basically any living creature

His hunger had no end---he would consume anyone who summoned him or made the mistake of crossing his path

But even evil has a purpose, and now Abadon would find his

The black-winged crusader broke the holy bonds that imprisoned Abadon at the bottom of the ancient lake of fire and brimstone

Abadon found himself free---free after an eternity of imprisonment in the lowest depths of the oceans of hell

He rose to the surface with a vengeance and sprang onto the brimstone island of hell

He planted himself in the middle of the city and anchored his feet into the brimstone

Then he grew into an ancient dragon, having such a height that his head was obscured by the dark, smoldering clouds of hell

He unhinged his jaw and let out a dark, ungodly, howling roar that echoed through all the planes of hell

"Now is the time of Abadon! Yield you spawns of hell and bow before me!

Bow before the king of the ancient dragons of hell!

Prepare to be consumed, you son of perdition, as I will consume you all---angels of hell and heaven alike!

I will consume your souls and black hearts into my mouth, and I don't repent, for one-by-one I'll gain all of the powers of hell and heaven!"

At first, the souls entered his mouth by the thousands, but then by the millions

He was inhaling all of the souls of hell into his infernal bowels and he began to digest them

He radiated with power, and hell wouldn't hold him for long

Soon he would hunger for angel's blood, but not only that, but for the blood of the Father, as well, who had cast him out

His bowels burned for vengeance against God, Lucifer, and more recently, man

He wanted to make the heavens themselves feel his suffering

He pulled the key to the bottomless pit from his neck and opened the smoldering abyss of hell

By the trillions, Abadon's army arose

They were in the form of locusts with stinging thorns at the base of their abdomens

They poured out onto the earth as a wine of wrath

Abadon howled with laughter

"Come you demons---hell is mine!

I shall consume you all!

Unshaken, the black-winged angel stood beside the fearful faceless man

Abadon was a titan whose size was dwarfed only by God himself

How could he be controlled and to what final purpose did he serve?

The faithless would soon see the truth of the cross

The leaders of the world would see the end of their reign of propaganda and war, intermixed with religion

Their time was at an end

The truth wouldn't be hidden any longer

Its horrors would be seen and its beauty would be revealed

The revelations found in the infinite blood of words and knowledge would carry the cross of truth and light

Then a blue-winged angel flew across the great abyss of the multiverse

She sat down upon the rings of Saturn and began to sing a song in tribute to all of the faithful souls that had gone unsung

Then there came the strange melody of a fiddle, the tone of which was created by the calls of ravens and the sound of which poured out onto the cemeteries of the earth

The ravens began to call the dead from their graves

Death opened up and all of the souls of her lovers poured out upon the great multiverse

Their lifeforce began to glow with a blue, ultra-violet light

An eerie fire danced about the dead and began to erupt in the sky

All of the earth sat in wonder

Lost souls emerged from their crypts

They came slowly at first---then in rivers--- then in oceans

They were crossing the great void of time and space

Dimensions opened into a loop of parallel worlds

They began folding in upon themselves as they ripped the very fabric of reality

It was an expansive purgatory that was becoming illuminated by a vast twilight of ancient souls

The dead mingled with unknown entities from dimensions both dark and forboding, all from the multiverse we thought we knew

There is a reason to fear the night, for its darkness holds the secrets of the unknown

Our own nightmares feed it, for the horrors of our worst-imagined terrors are given life in our minds and souls

Some of us are haunted by an eternity of "living within a dream within a dream" (as it's been said),---an endless nightmare from which there's no escape

Yet death found a softness in her heart and she would free us by the will of God

A new world was coming, forged by all of the powers of creation

A place where all forms of life could exist

A place where darkness and light would become one

And the dead were being drawn into this new creation---a world where all dimensions meet and all doors are open

The black-winged angel charged to the heavens to see this procession of the dead and to become a witness to this new world of balance---a realm where good and evil serve the same purpose

For all of Lucifer's works, terrible as they may be, still serve God's will and his mysterious ways

Now the black-winged angel would become a union of balance for good and evil

He would make the shadows and the light one

Lifetime after lifetime, all passing by to this point in time, down to this one grain of sand from the hourglass of eternity

The black-winged angel is rising---give ear to the one called Melancholia!

His tears of sadness and repentance had touched God's heart enough to allow him back into his holy presence

Now he would become a symbol of God's mercy and a servant of God's will

For who could know joy without the wisdom of sadness?

Chaos and order would find their purpose beside one another

The universe is boundless, but it does have laws that even God himself must live by, or how could he be God?

The way is through the word of light and truth

Light and truth are the creators of law, ordained by the ancient decree of righteousness

These demons were originally the children of God, but some of God's children had become abominations

These were the darkest souls that left the eternal abyss of oblivion

Through the blackest of hell's catacombs they fled

They didn't fear a second fall or a worse oblivion

They sought only death and their own extinction, for bitter is the wine of regret

They thirsted for revenge for their banishment

Their spirits imparted anguish as they walked among us, seeking to destroy us from within

They hated all of God's living creations

When one gazes upon the stars, true darkness can't be seen

It must be felt to truly know its horror

So many souls are lost to the infernal darkness

They build their prisons brick-by-brick

Screams of agony and woe become their only remaining offerings

It was time for Abadon to consume hell and all its children of true darkness

But now the black-winged angel called Melancholia understood---he would save all the souls of sorrow and the truly repentant, and leave Lucifer and Abadon to their own devices to battle each other for the rule of hell for all eternity

The angry roar of Lucifer could be heard throughout the multiverse as he discovered Abadon destroying his kingdom of abomination

They locked themselves into a death embrace and began to wage a battle with each other the likes of which had not been seen since the first war of heaven

Lucifer plunged his horns into the behemoth's chest, and when he withdrew his head, the horns remained

Lucifer then drew his sword of unholy darkness, but Abadon cast him across the throne room and charged into his body with such force that Lucifer became pinned against his throne

Lucifer laughed in pain and wounded self-pride

He raised his sword and castrated Abadon even while his horns were still stuck in Abadon's chest

Abadon let out a great, howling bellow

It echoed out from hell all the way to the heavens

Abadon then covered Lucifer in a breath of hellfire and brimstone

Even Lucifer was driven back by these cosmic fires of hell and damnation

It was the breath of a dragon who was so ancient and forgotten, and it was the breath of the lake of fire

For the first time since his great fall, Lucifer felt fear rather than his eternal pride

Before now, he had taken such pride in his wits, but now they might not be enough to save him

He hurled himself with all of his powers of darkness at Abadon and thrust his blade deep into the spine of the ancient dragon

Abadon staggered for a moment, as fiery blood poured out over his wounds, and he groaned with pain and anger

He ripped the sword from his spine and impaled Lucifer upon his throne with it

Abadon laughed with a darkness and yelled, "Now you can reign upon your throne forever!"

Lucifer grabbed his sword with his hands and struggled to free himself from his impalement

"Now you shall learn why they call me the son of perdition!", he shouted

He conjured a golden trident from his throne and cast it into Abadon's heart

All the fires of hell engulfed the throne room as Abadon fell to his knees

He slowly pulled the trident from his heart and struggled to cast it back as Lucifer

The trident struck Lucifer in the abdomen and held him fast against the throne once more

Abadon regained his footing and began charging towards him

Then demons from all of the corners of hell came to protect their injured prince of darkness

They came with shields and swords made from a metal unfathomably strong and unknown to man

They encircled Abadon in a flanking maneuver and began to move forward

Abadon screamed out and from his mouth an ocean of stinging locusts streamed out

The locusts began to devour the demons

Lucifer spoke out a word of power that hadn't been uttered since the first war in heaven

He spoke a secret chant that shook the very foundations of hell and the whole multiverse itself

The spell sent the locusts away to feast on the souls of men

As his servants were being consumed, Lucifer had grown in power

Then he seemed to bend time and fly away from the legions that were protecting him in battle

It was chaos---it was life and death married in a carnal, epic struggle

It was a war against all life itself

Which would it be, life or death that would survive and win the unknown God's favor?

The black-winged crusader came-to in the smoldering clouds

The whole of heaven and earth glowed in a strange blue fire

It was the rising of a sun that began eclipsing a terrible blue-maroon moon behind it

The black-winged angel's eyes locked with Lucifer's and they began to talk in an ancient tongue unknown to all of man

Together they weighed the balance of what was to come from their war---the cost that would have to be paid

They debated tactics and discussed the lost lives and where they would go, as if they were discussing a cosmic chess game with man stuck in the middle

There was a terrible trembling of lightning and tornadoes joined together---the earth smoldered and shook

There was a terrible darkness through which none could see

Through the blackness, a lonely, blue, fiery tear ran down the face of the one called Melancholia, who was doomed to know the fate of the entire multiverse and the suffering of all life

It's easy to focus on his transgressions that are both ancient and unspoken of for eternities, but no one knows of the beauty that he had seen in the beginning of time, before life had flooded the multiverse

He had stood in the presence of the unknown God, being protected by the wings of angels

He was the unknown God's mystery, and only the son of God knew his secrets

He was a witness of all creation

He had buried himself in a library of books, texts, and ancient scrolls

He had an unmeasurable hunger for knowledge and wisdom

As a result of having been in the full divine presence of the unknown God, he had been set afire by thought and wonder

For not even he could be shielded by the blinding light and power that radiated from the unknown God's eyes

But to be in the unknown God's heart was to know all of the mysteries of creation

God had such a reverence for life that he gave it a choice, or what some would call free will

One might say he truly loves life in all its forms

The war in heaven darkened his heart

He had witnessed the atrocities of war in God's kingdom, as brother slew brother in an ocean of angelic blood

His wrath pushed at him to destroy them all, but in his noble divinity, God softened before he acted, and cast out the ones called to the nephilim---the fallen angels of all the heavens

The black-winged crusader had seen the unknown God stand motionless, frozen in grief

The black-winged crusader had been forbidden by God to fight, and his hunger to preserve life drove him mad

He lost his mind to the echoes of dying voices and angelic moans

He had known them all since the birth of time

Eventually, he couldn't hold back his sword any longer, and he drove it into the deepest legions of the rebel angels, and shed his first angry drops of angelic blood

Tears fell down his face as he stood in the pyrrhic battle that had split creation in two

Life and death would now be forever intertwined in a circle of suffering and doubt, and only the bold could now dare to make a stand in the aftermath of God's loss of the eternal peace of heaven

The whole multiverse of dimensions had lost its virginity to the birth of war

Oh what a terrible dark bird she is, war, consuming all that she encounters in an ocean of fire and death

And yet the one called Melancholia stood on the edge of oblivion again, for war never really dies, it just changes battlefields

And this war could destroy the multiverse and all the life that dwelled within it

Given the chance, the over-friendly angels of despair would snuff us out like a dying candle

The blue eerie flames engulfed Melancholia as he asked Lucifer to yield

He asked him to end the battle

The dark-winged crusader didn't want to provide a birthplace for the coming dogs of war

He pleaded with Lucifer to cease the battle, and reminded him of the countless brothers they had lost in Lucifer's rage of abandon

But Lucifer couldn't repent---his pride's ego had placed him in the chains of his own eternal woe

He would serve God's purpose without even having knowledge of it, and his chains wouldn't be loosened

Lucifer had cast the die for open war

The black-winged angel disappeared into the cosmos

The ancient one called Melancholia prayed out across the multiverse for the unknown God's direction, for this time he had steeled himself in his anger and obedience to the glory of God, whom he had once betrayed, and had done what he had been forbidden to do

Then, through the mystery of God, Melancholia was restored with the grace he had lost, and God showed him how to win this hell-borne war of attrition

The black-winged angel called Melancholia cried out with the roar of a lion over his soul's lost unity with God and then began chanting a secret prayer

It echoed out across the horizon in an ancient tongue

It contained the riddle of life and death, and it spoke with great waves of ancient dialect

It became alive, and spheres of fiery, ultra-blue light glowed out across all of time and existence

It stopped the grains of the multiverse's hourglass in mid-pour---the sands just froze over

The son of the unknown God appeared in the many heavens

He had a strange new crown upon his head, with a name upon it that no one could read

He became entangled with the holy spirit of life, and began to chant sacramental prayers across the multiverse

These were prayers that mortal man could never even dream of imagining

The prayers sprang to life giving a glow to the heavens

The son of God had heard Melancholia's sigh from across the multiverse

It had echoed even unto the throne of the unknown God himself

The son of God had come to calm the black-winged angel and to answer his prayers

He took him back to the garden of Eden and showed him the beauty of the world before it was corrupted, and he told him it would be pure again

The son of God showed him what he had fought for

He showed him an ocean of tears and the endless cycle of black and blue marks upon all of the creations of the Lord

The son of the unknown God poured out the blood-wine of wrath upon Melancholia and the heavens

The moon of the earth flickered in the blue ultra-violet flames of the crown of the Lord

The son of God stood before the whole multiverse and every dimension bowed before the holy spirit, pouring out the grail of his heart which is of the last cup that gives eternal life

The son of God drank in the spirit of life that is eternal and it shall not be snuffed out by the will of hopelessness or darkness

Knowledge poured out into the hearts of the living and these newly wise became thankful for their faith in the unknown God that had seen them through life eternal

The clock was very late in its hour of action

The will of God was upon us

The four horseman of the apocalypse were standing in their instance

All marveled at the stars as they witnessed the great horror that would have its day

The moment of time had come for great powers of epic proportions to clash in an infinite battle

Strange ancient spirits rose to see the hourglass of oblivion whose sands were running out

A dry, smiling, weeping was upon the dark-winged angel

The madness of his spirit burned with the stomach of famine, but he was healed by the grace of the unknown God

Magical, mystic legends poured out upon the cities of the forgotten fields

The earth was trembling in its wake

The jester of hell rose onto the land with illusion and glamour to blind all who were not faithful to the unknown God

A great tower rose up from the ground to the sky, but in time it became fallen

Kings were now humbled by the emptiness of their treasures

Death had been their only prophet and messiah

Now in the new world order of war, armed with their famine and disease, the false kings come for all souls in their lust for wealth and power

Melancholia was soon returned from Eden to rise upon the battlefield

The holy power of smite was gifted to him by the son of God

The ancient legendary hammer of smite could turn the tides of war

He flew with cosmic speed and smashed this holy relic upon the unholy battlefield, smiting all the wicked souls that stood upon the planes of existence

Angels, demons, and men cried out to the heavens, asking God for the battle to end before it had even begun

Melancholia knew the cost of the war, and it therefore placed his mind in a sublime state of eternal sorrow

He had shed the blood of his brothers before in the war of heaven

It was there in the third heaven that his guilt weighed heavy upon his heart

He prayed to the unknown God, praying that this day would pass him by

But that couldn't be, for he had a debt to pay, for the blood that he had spilled in heaven was upon his head, and its horrors couldn't be shaken

What lone human could fathom the weight of such cosmic justice that had played out across the faces of eternity?

The black-winged angel sighed out in a wailing howl

His heart felt the ancient conflict of thought, as before when he had driven Azzal back from the gates of heaven

The sight of blood was a dark omen

The faces of the damned stretched out across horizon after horizon

So much blood had been spilled in the name of the unknown God

How could anyone remain standing in such a sublime sorrow?

It was a story so sad that it should never be told, for it would surely drive most to madness

In the wake of birth comes the acknowledgement of death, thus the black-wing of heaven was driven mad by the epic pain of immortality

He knew too much for his own sanity to be able to withstand

With such visions of prophecy, he wailed for his memory to be lost to time

That's why God had granted him his wish to forget

Within a foggy dream in the back of his mind he finally remembered a clue to his divine ancestry

His memory was the source of his great sorrow

God has seen his true regret and had plucked him from the gates of hell

He had been in the void called purgatory for one hundred thousand years

Waiting in limbo for this moment which was truly a chance at divine redemption

It had been a noble honor to be in the presence of God

And now the wisdom of the eternal poured out across the sky, embracing him

With his restored grace he could feel the power of truth and righteousness

The sorrow of his mind washed away into the voids of time

He rose from his prayer and stood, saying, "Oh God of Gods, oh God of fire and wind and air, I call upon your ancient hand to guide me, Father

I remember you---I remember the heavens---I remember your glory

Send me Father to avenge you"

He flew with cosmic speed to the battlefield and began to turn the tides of war, from the shadows to the light

He single-handedly broke through the lines to confront the knights of gloom and death with the steel of his sword that couldn't be broken

Spirit after spirit fell back again to the darkness that they had once escaped

The spirit of the unknown God was upon him now

He could feel the divinity coursing through his veins, providing him with the strength of the unknown God

His body pulsed with the energy of a sun about to go super-nova

All of hell was upon him, for their attention had been turned by his hand

Now they attacked him like angry hornets

He was swallowed up by the darkest angels of hell on all sides

His enemies challenged him from the shadows of earth, all the way to the craters of the moon

But he wouldn't yield in his attack, nor submit to doubt

His grace had returned, filling his spirit with strength

The son of the unknown God poured out his grail of the blood of wrath upon him for the third and final time

And the wake of the blood left an ocean of dead whose lives wouldn't be restored after judgment day occurs

The hand of the unknown God was upon them

He shook the heavens to and fro, as a great earthquake

Demons poured out of every plane of existence

The cosmos shook as dimensions collided

The heavens rumbled with a dark energy

Now the son of shadow and light called Melancholia glowed with power

The heralds of hell engulfed him in fire and brimstone

His eyes were aglow with raw power as the demons' flames embraced him

In a cosmic-blue glint, the halo that adorned him as a crown shined with ultra-violet blue flames

It glowed with the brilliance of a sun, blinding the legions of hell and atomizing them in flames of the bluest hue

They burned in agony as the full sword of oblivion fell down upon them, causing their existence to cease

They had been burned away from the book of life completely, never to return

The earth smoked and clouded over as the weight of man was put to the scales of divine justice

The heavens fell quiet with wonder and, at last, the truth of peace raised its flag upon the whole of existence

And for one instant, the multiverse observed a moment of silence for the Lord of lords and the King of kings

All hail the unknown son of God!

"Let us start anew", the unknown God commanded

And he again began to create new worlds and new life

For the time of truth had come

www.ingramcontent.com/pod-product-compliance
Lightning Source LLC
Chambersburg PA
CBHW081346070526
44578CB00005B/739